"Deidra listens not quite like anyone else I've ever met. She listens to hearts—to wandering, wondering, wounded ones—and then intimately to the heart of God. And because Deidra lets herself become all ear, she is a rare, wise soul, uniquely positioned to voice what our souls are most hungry for and usher us directly into a veritable fresh and satisfying feast, the glory of it running down the sides of our questions and fears."

from the foreword by Ann Voskamp,
author of the *New York Times* bestsellers
One Thousand Gifts and *The Greatest Gift*

"Deidra is a leader among leaders. She tenderly but swiftly leads people to Jesus and to a better understanding of themselves."

Jennie Allen, founder and visionary of IF:Gathering;
author of *Restless* and *Anything*

"With her signature wisdom and wit, Deidra Riggs is the friend we need to tell us we don't have to try so hard. To help us see how 'every little thing we do' matters. Every conversation. Every encounter. Every mundane and meaningful activity. Every mistake and regret. God will use 'every little thing in our lives, and in this book, to reveal his grace to us and through us. I can't wait to give it as a gift to family and friends!"

Renee Swope, bestselling author of *A Confident Heart*

"This is a book for those of us who wonder if God still changes the world through ordinary people. It's a book that reminds us that God is active and creatively at work in the commuter lane, in the cubicles, and at 2:00 a.m. in between sick kids and our own fearful souls. If you've ever wondered if God's grand promises extend beyond the pages of Scripture and into our everyday lives, this is a book for you. Deidra's words have given me fresh eyes to look for God's faithful fulfillment of his promises in the nooks and crannies of my own very ordinary life, and to be listening for his deliberate 'Let there be . . .' as he creates a universe of purpose around and through each one of us."

Lisa-Jo Baker, author of *Surprised by Motherhood*;
community manager for (in)courage

"If you've ever quietly wondered, 'Is this all there is?' then Deidra Riggs wants to invite you on an intimate adventure with Jesus. Her gentle, challenging words will open your eyes to the extraordinary right in the middle of your ordinary and guide you toward a deeper, wilder sense of purpose and joy."

Holley Gerth, *Wall Street Journal* bestselling author
of *You're Loved No Matter What*

"If you've ever thought that you aren't one of the world changers, get ready to be proven wrong. With a mix of story and Scripture, Deidra invites us into the adventure of living every little moment of our lives with God."

Sarah Bessey, author of *Jesus Feminist* and *Out of Sorts*

every little thing

Making a World of Difference
Right Where You Are

deidra riggs

BakerBooks

a division of Baker Publishing Group
Grand Rapids, Michigan

© 2015 by Deidra Riggs

Published by Baker Books
a division of Baker Publishing Group
P.O. Box 6287, Grand Rapids, MI 49516-6287
www.bakerbooks.com

Printed in the United States of America

Library of Congress Cataloging-in-Publication Data
Riggs, Deidra, 1964–
    Every little thing : making a world of difference right where you are / Deidra Riggs.
        pages cm
    Includes bibliographical references.
    ISBN 978-0-8010-1842-8 (pbk.)
    1. Christian women—Religious life. I. Title.
BV4527.R555 2015
248.8′43—dc23   2015016589

The author is represented by William K. Jensen Literary Agency, 119 Bampton Court, Eugene, Oregon 97404.

In keeping with biblical principles of creation stewardship, Baker Publishing Group advocates the responsible use of our natural resources. As a member of the Green Press Initiative, our company uses recycled paper when possible. The text paper of this book is composed in part of post-consumer waste.

15 16 17 18 19 20 21   7 6 5 4 3 2 1

To Nano and Popo

You loved me, right from the start.

Contents

Foreword by Ann Voskamp   9

Part 1 Knowing Yourself

Introduction   15

1. When You Miss the Mark   27
2. The Cherry Tree Has Got to Go   43
3. The Opposite of Fear   57

Part 2 Following God's Leading

4. You Want Me to Go Where?   77
5. Breathlessness   99
6. Pay Attention   113

Part 3 Taking the Next Step

7. The Gospel Needs to Be Lived   127
8. Every Little Thing   141
9. We Are the Lucky Ones   161

Acknowledgments   181
Notes   187

Foreword

Marjorie Knight told me when I wasn't quite yet nine.

She turned to me while we were hulling a heap of strawberries over her sink. Her white hair caught all this afternoon light. And her gravelly voice rolled over those words like smoothened stones:

"Running hard after an extraordinary life turns out to be chasing a lie. The realest extraordinary is always found in the ordinary. That extra everyone's looking for? It's found in ordinary."

She didn't say much after that, but I tasted her words in the strawberries she gave me, in the swallowing down of the rubies, the glory of them running out the side of the mouth.

I'm half the age of Marjorie before I deeply understand how sunlight can warm anyone's face when you take time to smile and give them an ear. That anyone can make a difference for all eternity—if they believe that it all counts, that it all matters—that it all, everything, can be the beginning of a widening, expansive miracle.

True, you won't read it as a headline in *People* magazine. But it is what the heroic people know: that glossy red carpets can lead to nowhere, and that the ordinary is the everyday container that holds *the realest extraordinary.*

That everyone single one of us gets eyes to look into, and people to touch, and light to give, and hands to reach out to, and igniting change to our own sacred corners of a waiting, broken world—and it's precisely because we feel small that we can walk through the world's broken cracks and get to the heart of people and make a difference.

The ordinary becomes the extraordinary when the eyes see the extra glory here. The ordinary becomes the extraordinary when our eyes see the extra glory of God right here where we are, moving and shaping and strengthening and rebuilding and redeeming and changing and resurrecting—and when our feet step into what God's doing right where we are.

There's nothing in this world that's normal—there's only growing blind to the glory.

It's a ridiculously free world. Everyone gets to accept the invitation of extraordinary into their ordinary or not.

Deidra Riggs is one astonishing woman whose life bears witness to just this. I've leaned across a table and listened to the winsome wisdom of this woman turn a key and unlock a door to more—*unlock something in me.*

Deidra listens not quite like anyone else I've ever met. She listens to hearts—to wandering, wondering, wounded ones—and then intimately to the heart of God. And because Deidra lets herself become all ear, she is a rare, wise soul, uniquely positioned to voice what our souls are most hungry for and usher us directly into a veritable fresh and satisfying feast, the glory of it running down the sides of our questions and fears.

Deidra said it once to me and I've never forgotten it: "We get to be terrified, so God gets to be glorified."

We get to jump tandem with God into the unknown, we get to break free of our comfort zones, we get to be the lucky ones who live large right where we are—*we get to be terrified—so God gets glorified.*

We get to look squarely at our lives and realize: We don't need more things. We need more *meaning* in everything.

And that meaning in our lives that we yearn for, it unfolds in our ordinary, when we get up every day with just a refrain of three lines:

The Extraordinary is *here.*

Because *God. is. here.*

So how can I say yes to the Extraordinary he's doing *right here?*

Because the gospel needs us to do more than only believe in it—*it asks us to be living it.*

Because you doing the next thing is The Next Big Thing that has a literal domino-effect, forever-effect in the kingdom of God.

Because how you courageously live your every days can make a world of people *taste* and *see* that the Lord, that life, that this world of making a difference, is good.

This is no small thing.

This is an *extraordinary* thing.

This can be your ordinary thing.

Just by the way you do *every little thing.*

Ann Voskamp, www.aholyexperience.com
and author of the *New York Times* bestsellers
One Thousand Gifts and *The Greatest Gift*
The Farm, Canada, Spring 2015

Part 1

Knowing Yourself

Introduction

I had always dreamed of jumping out of an airplane. So when I finally got the chance, I didn't have one ounce of fear.

It was a beautiful fall morning in Pennsylvania, and I woke up early to make the ninety-minute drive to New Jersey where I was to attend "jump school." Only my husband knew about my adventure. There was, I reasoned, no need to cause anyone concern. I'd be home safe and sound before most people had eaten their breakfast and finished their Saturday morning chores.

On that Saturday morning, I pointed my car east and drove toward the culmination of a dream I'd been nursing for a very long while. I don't know where or what or who first got me started dreaming about jumping from an airplane with a parachute strapped to my back. I really have no reason to want to do something like that. I mean, I do like adventure, but I don't like roller coasters. No one in my family—not my parents or my sister—rides roller coasters. The idea of riding the rails at a local theme park is enough to turn my knees to jelly. I guess I like a certain genre of adventure. Parasailing?

Check. Swimming with the dolphins? Check. Skydiving? Yes, please.

When I tell people I jumped out of an airplane, someone inevitably asks, "On purpose?" Ha! Of course it was on purpose.

Naturally, I wasn't by myself. The jump I took was a tandem jump with a skilled and experienced skydiver. When I pulled into the parking lot of that jump school, I felt absolutely giddy with excitement. I parked the car and locked it, and I made my way to the office to check in and get my instructions.

There were about twelve of us jumping that morning. Double that when you include the professionals who would welcome us on their own thrill-seeking adventures, our tandem guides. We signed a lot of papers in the office, saying we wouldn't blame anyone but ourselves if our adventure that day ended in anything but success. That was saying a lot, because failure at skydiving really isn't an option. Then all of us were ushered into a tiny room where we stood behind a rail and watched a video about skydiving, the risks and the joys. We were then led out to the hangar, where we received our instructions. I was told that when the time came to jump out of the plane, I should spread my arms and legs wide and lift up my chin. That was about it. Our instruction session lasted about ten minutes and gave us just enough information to know this was probably a little bit risky but definitely a whole lot of fun.

After our jump school training, we were each given a harness, and an attendant helped make sure we were properly fitted and locked in. Then we were assigned a jump expert—an actual skydiver! I wish I could remember my guy's name. He was the coolest. He had bright white hair and skin that was nearly translucent. His eyes were hidden behind reflective sunglasses that wrapped around his spiked and gelled hair, and he wore a jumpsuit that was mostly white with a few touches of color added for flair. For our purposes, let's call him "my guy."

My guy handed me an altimeter. Everyone got one. We were told to wear the altimeter on our wrist like a watch. All around the face of the altimeter were numbers, and a dial in the center would serve the purpose of keeping track of just how far we fell from the sky once we jumped out of the plane. My guy tapped a red arrow on my altimeter and said, "When we reach this altitude, that's when I'll pull the rip cord."

I looked at the red arrow, and then I looked up at him, shaking my head. "Oh no," I said with a wave of my hand and hint of bravado (okay, probably more than a hint), "I'm going to pull the cord. I've been looking forward to this for so long!"

My guy tucked his chin in toward his shoulder, and I saw his eyebrows rise over the tops of his sunglasses. Was that a smile? I couldn't be sure. "Are you sure?" he asked.

"Definitely!" I said.

He didn't try to make me change my mind. He didn't try to convince me to reconsider. He simply said, "Okay." Then he stood behind me, as if we were already strapped together, and gave me rip cord pulling instructions, which went like this: "When we get to that arrow, reach down with your right hand and pull the cord. I'll see you up there!" And then he was gone, boosting my confidence that much further. If I had something to be concerned about, he'd have stuck around, either to convince me to change my mind or to make sure I knew what I was doing. Right?

The next time I saw my guy was when we were all headed to the airplane on the tarmac. It was a small propeller plane, and he stood at the door and saluted me, then hopped into the plane ahead of me. On the plane, we sat on the floor, scooched up very closely to one another, single file. I sat right in front of my guy, and he hooked our harnesses together with heavy-duty carabiner hooks, and not long after that the plane took off.

We climbed in wide, loopy circles up into the clouds, and I watched the airstrip and the jump school and the autumn leaves in the trees get smaller and smaller through the little airplane window at my shoulder. I was still giddy. I don't know that I can say the same about the rest of the people on the plane. I wasn't really paying attention to them.

When the plane reached whatever altitude is the right altitude for jumping, one of the skydivers stood up and opened the door—something I'd never seen happen before on an airplane. The door was like an overhead garage door that rolled up into the top of the plane, and I caught a glimpse of the sky.

I would be the second to jump. Well, me and my guy. The first to jump was someone who'd done this before. He was performing his very first solo jump, along with his jump instructor. They stood at that wide-open door. They counted to three. Then they just fell away. But because the airplane was moving at the same time they fell away from us, from where I sat, it looked as if they simply disappeared. Gone. Into thin air.

My guy tapped me on my shoulder and said into my ear, "I want you to slide down there and sit on the edge and wrap your legs around the plane." That, right there, was the first time I thought to myself, "Hmmm. That's not something you hear every day." I followed his instructions and slid myself down to the edge and wrapped my legs around the plane. My guy said, "Remember to lift your chin," and the next thing I

18

knew, we were falling through the sky. *Hurtling* is probably a better word.

I could not catch my breath or close my lips around my teeth. The hood of my jacket flapped around like a bird trapped in a wood-burning stove. My throat closed up and threatened to suffocate me.

I was having a blast. Oh my goodness, what a rush!

When the parachute opened over our heads, there was nothing but silence. Well, silence and the sound of my ear-piercing screams. But once I calmed down, there was silence. Suspended in the air, I took in the beauty of it all. The sky above. The autumn colors below. The fact that I'd just jumped out of a plane. Even the rainbow-colored canopy was a gift in that moment—not just because it was keeping us from catastrophe but also because of its beauty. Finally, I found some words, and I thanked my guy for the jump and for this moment as I kept marveling at the beauty surrounding us both. He agreed. "It really is an incredible thing. Not very many people get to do something like this," he said.

Our landing was perfect, and when my feet touched the earth, I could not have been more excited. My guy and I high-fived each other. We did the bump. We hugged. And do you know what he said to me? He said, "Deidra! You're a skydiver now!"

Me. A skydiver.

Eventually, I made my way back to my car and began driving west, back toward home. It took a long time to recover from such an adrenaline rush, but I could feel that I was slowly coming back to myself as I drove the car down the road.

About forty-five minutes into the drive home, however, I had an epiphany. Is that the right word? Perhaps it would be better to say that I arrived at a terrifying realization. It was a realization that brought me right back to reality and sent me veering off the road and onto the shoulder. I realized that I never pulled the rip cord!

Egads!

As I sat there on the side of the highway, my breath came in gasps and my chest heaved up and down with the horror of it all. I, with my arrogant bravado—waving my guy off and telling him I'd take care of pulling the rip cord—didn't pull the rip cord. Oh my goodness, I would have killed us both!

I began to cry. I considered turning the car around to apologize to my guy for almost ending his skydiving career for good. I was mortified. I was terribly embarrassed. I was so very thankful to be alive and to know that my guy was alive and well, probably jumping out of another plane at that very moment. "Good grief, God!" I cried out. "How in the world do you put up with me? Thank you, thank you, thank you," I told him, "for saving our lives today!"

Do you know what happened next? Right in that moment, on the side of the road, I realized that my guy was a lot like God. My guy was going to jump whether I went with him or not. He lived for days like these, when the breeze was still and the sky was clear. On this particular day, my guy had been kind enough to let me join him on his first jump of the day. And when I got all arrogant and proud (right in his face, to boot!), he took it all in stride. Because he knew the deal. He knew that if I flubbed it, he had everything under control.

We have video of that jump I took. In the video you can see when we reach the point in our jump where the hand of the altimeter rested on the red arrow. My guy pulls my arm in front of me and points to the altimeter, and I give him no response. Just my cheeks pressed up against my eyeballs and my lips pulled away from my teeth. Then my guy reaches around and taps me on my forehead. Nothing. So my guy points to the cameraman, gives a thumbs-up sign, reaches for the rip cord with his right hand, just as I was supposed to have done, and away we go as the canopy unfurls over our heads and sweeps us up into the sky.

After all of that, my guy never mentioned my mistake. He didn't point his finger at me once we reached the ground and say, "You almost killed us both! You never pulled the cord!" While we were suspended in the air, he never said, "What were you thinking?" And when our feet touched the ground, my guy gave me a high five, he bumped hips with me, and then, as the icing on the cake, my guy called me a skydiver.

Me. A skydiver. Now, you and I both know I am far from a skydiver. But like I said, my guy was a lot like God that day. God, who isn't afraid of adventure. God, who is going to do something incredible despite us. God, who invites us to join him on the journey and the adventure of a lifetime. He doesn't point his finger at us and count all the ways we mess up. Not even when we think we've got it all under control and we tell him so.

Sometimes our dreams are like that. They are big, and we approach them with bravado and tell God we'll take it from here. Thank God for grace. It covers us in situations such as these, like a brightly colored canopy unfurled over us before we realize just how badly we need it and how out of control we really are.

God's grace covers us in the little things as well. No life is so small that God doesn't notice it. No act of worship escapes his view. Who cares if we've got all the edges smoothed out? Even when we miss the mark and we get too big for our britches, God is there. He has a plan for us, and he delights in us. God is perfectly capable of handling it all (and then some) on his own, but—and this just blows my mind—he chooses to invite us to join him, even before we know what we're doing and before we've gotten our act together.

That, my friend, is the message of this book.

God has designs on us (see Gal. 1:15)—plans to use us—and in this case the proof of that is the book you now hold in your hands. I never thought or intended or dreamed that a single person in this world would buy a book I'd written. But saying that is a bit misleading—as if I'd actually even considered a scenario in which someone else would read my writing.

I hadn't. As far as I was concerned, there are writers, and there are readers. That, my friends, is the circle of literary life as I understood it. We need each other, and I am more than happy to fulfill the role of the introverted and slightly nerdy bookworm, curled up on the corner of a well-loved couch cushion with a dog-eared book in my hand.

As it turns out, God knows us well.

He knows the way you're wired. He knows the things that scare you. He's not surprised by your rough edges. He doesn't blink twice when you insert your foot in your mouth or miss an opportunity to point someone his way. He knows what you've already decided you aren't.

How about that? Which jobs have you crossed off because you don't have the time, the experience, or the resources? Which adventure is God trying to get on your calendar, but you keep deleting it because you're not as smart as so-and-so, or because that adventure doesn't fit inside your comfort zone, or because you'd just rather not, thank you very much?

I don't think there's a person among us who doesn't want his or her life to make a difference. We see a need in our church, our school, our neighborhood, our family, the world. We look at it and think, *Someone really should get to work on that.* Then we wait for the next great someone to show up, take matters into her own hands, and change the situation—change the world. Because, really, who are we?

We are "just" the car pool lane sitters, the diaper changers, the dish washers, the cubicle workers, the second-job holders, the lawn mowers, the pancake flippers, the rule followers, the occasional Sunday morning churchgoers, the Saturday night Netflixers, the Facebook status updaters, the one-mile joggers, the regular everyday ordinary us.

We are not the world changers. That's a job for someone else. Someone with more moxie, more wisdom, more knowledge, more humor, more skill, more subscribers, a bigger platform, a better marriage, a fancier vehicle, a more gorgeous headshot, letters after her name, multiple speaking gigs, a perfect manicure, and an organic garden in her suburban backyard.

But isn't that what Gideon thought? When that angel looked at Gideon and pronounced him a mighty warrior (see Judg. 6), I imagine Gideon pointing his index finger to his heart and looking over his shoulder before looking back at that angel to mouth the words, "Who? Me?" God sees something in us that doesn't reflect in a mirror. It's the person God knows we can be when we surrender our lives to him. And that person? That person is a world changer.

Maybe you're the one who sees a need, and you might even see the solution. But somehow you're convinced you couldn't possibly be the person for *that* job. If you entertain the dreams God placed on your heart and wonder how you'll ever find the time, the space, the audience, the resources to make that dream come true, this book was written for you. You are my soul sister.

Perhaps you're convinced your life is lackluster and insignificant. People ask what you do, and your response begins with "Just . . . ," and you stifle a sigh when you're done speaking the words. You feel like a closet wallflower and a self-doubter, an expert comparer. You never measure up. You feel as if you cower in caves instead of toppling injustice, while constantly shushing the desire in your heart to see someone—*anyone*—make a difference in places no one else seems to notice. This book is for you too. I have carved my name into the walls of that very same cave.

God has a different message to share with us. The job God has given us isn't about *fixing* anything. It's about surrendering every part of me to all of him. Changing the world isn't the same as fixing it. The world has already been fixed; it has already been saved. And changing the world doesn't mean one woman, all by herself. Changing the world is about each individual member of the body of Christ recognizing the sacredness of the role we play in the places we find ourselves every day, even if our place is in the car pool lane instead of the marble halls of justice or the towering pulpit of a megachurch.

Most of us will make a difference in this world, but not because of some grand or large-scale initiative. No, most of us will change our corner of the world and make an impact that stands the test of time through the small and seemingly insignificant (to us) interactions and decisions and conversations of our average days. We make a difference where we live, and incrementally, that place begins to shift. But the first and most important shift takes place on the inside, in all those places that rise up within, making you point to your heart, look over your shoulder, and then mouth the words, "Who? Me?"

This book is your invitation to celebrate that journey. Celebrating the significance of this one, ordinary, average life shifts our perspective and starts us on the road to God's adventure for our lifetime. This book invites you to the celebration of every little thing that makes your life spectacularly breathtaking and of the fulfillment of all God has in store. It's a book that climbs down from the high and lofty and that quietly shuts a door against the clamoring and clanging and striving and trying to be heard above the noise. It's not a book written because I've figured out all the answers to all the questions. It's not a list of items you can check off and know you've changed the world. This book is my story of a heart turned inside out, a faith that lost its footing and scrambled up for one last gasp of air. It is the story of finding myself at the bottom of a drought-stricken gully, praying for someone to make it rain, and discovering a swollen drop of water at the bottom of a dusty Styrofoam cup. A cup, I realized, I'd been holding in my hand all along.

This book is the story of how God is in control of our lives, even when we think we've got things under control. It is also your encouragement that when God looks at you and you wonder if he really sees someone who can make a difference in this world, he looks you straight in the eyes and says, "Yes. You."

Keep your chin up. It's time to jump.

★★★★★★ *1* ★★★★★★

When You Miss the Mark

If you only look at us, you might well miss the brightness.
We carry this precious Message around in the unadorned
clay pots of our ordinary lives. That's to prevent anyone
from confusing God's incomparable power with us.

2 Corinthians 4:7

Sometimes I think the most holy place in the world is high
above the clouds in coach class. I think that now because
my children are adults and we hardly ever travel together
anymore. Not that I'd mind traveling with them, but they
are living their own lives and flying to their own adventures.
With adult children, I am free to sit back, relax, and enjoy
my flight without having to worry about whether they will
kick the seat of the passenger in front of me or scream at

unbearable decibel levels or blow out their diaper as soon as we reach a safe cruising altitude. I don't have to try to schedule my flights around nap time or balance a car seat and a stroller and a diaper bag on one hip and my beautiful, intelligent, screaming child on the other.

These days, I welcome a two-hour flight with nothing to do but read a good book, take a nap, or gaze out the portal into thin air. I watch the moms and dads carrying Superman backpacks as they make their way down the airplane aisle. They look hopeful, or haggard, or just trying to hold on. I try to make eye contact and smile, sending a silent wish of success toward them. Sometimes they see me, and their eyes betray their anxiety or their weariness or their belief that it will all go well. On a good day, I say a prayer for them because I remember exactly how it feels to board an airplane with a toddler and hope for the best.

But the truth is that not all of my days are good days.

Once I boarded a flight home after a fun visit to the East Coast. I'd spent a few days visiting my children in New York and Pennsylvania, and then I'd hung out in Virginia with my parents, my sister, and my sister's family.

In the Philadelphia airport, waiting for my flight home, I settled down in a seat near the gate to wait to board my flight. I hadn't been sitting there long when a young woman walked by rolling a stroller with a little blond-haired guy in the seat—all chilled out with his toddler lean. His mom sat down a few seats away from me and turned the stroller so Little Man was facing her. This mom was on it. She had snacks and little toys and books and diapers and wipes and, I imagine, a change of clothes for everyone, just in case.

She had it going on.

28

I listened to her talk to her son. His name, I discovered, was Max. Max's mom spoke in a voice that was calm, matter-of-fact, and reassuring. She and her guy in the stroller were clearly no strangers to the whole flying-on-an-airplane thing, and they were taking this entire event in stride. No stress. No crying. No impatient pacing or worried looks at her watch or at the gate. I took a sip of coffee from my cup and leaned back in my own seat. I wondered if Max's mom had taken lots of airplane trips with her own mom and was passing down a legacy of calm that Max would in turn pass along to his children.

Max was all smiles, and when we boarded the airplane, the flight attendants were instantly smitten. Max was indeed a charmer, an expert at melting the heart of anyone who looked in his direction.

Sitting down in my seat on the aisle, I buckled my seat belt and opened the book I was reading. Soon I was lost in the words on the page, and I didn't realize how long we'd been sitting there without moving.

In my experience, it's not usually a good thing when the airline captain announces he has "an update" to share. The captain said there was a minor maintenance issue, the mechanic was taking care of it, and we should be pushing back from the gate in just a few minutes. No biggie. I glanced up to see Max standing up in his mom's lap and the kind woman seated next to them engaged in animated conversation with Max. Everything was under control, so I went back to reading the book in my hands.

The words on the page were, as they say, ministering to my heart. I could practically reach out and touch God's love, right there in seat 14D. My soul was filled to overflowing with an overwhelming acknowledgment of the grace of God

29

and the beauty of the Word made flesh, and it was all I could do not to stand up and lead this planeload of travelers in a verse of "Amazing Grace."

But the captain's voice interrupted my sanctified moment, and this time he said, "Well, I have good news, and I have bad news." Not a good sign.

Turns out, the mechanic was able to fix the minor maintenance issue, but another malfunction had been discovered. Mechanics were bringing in the part from another airline, and they had every expectation they'd be able to fix it. We should be in the air in an hour.

A few passengers groaned aloud, and others pulled out their phones and began to look into making different travel arrangements. I assessed my own situation and realized I had no reason to hurry. I wasn't hungry, and I had a good book to read. On top of that, I wasn't traveling with children. Max had fallen asleep on his mom's lap.

An hour later, however, Max was awake and the captain was telling us events hadn't unfolded quite the way the mechanics had anticipated. The airplane was broken and we needed to get off.

Deplane.

Start over.

May I just tell you my traveling companions were not happy? Things quickly fell apart. Across the aisle, Max began to whimper.

Eventually, a new plane was brought to our gate, we were rebooked and reseated, and most of us filed on to the new plane to begin our adventure again. On this new plane, I had the same seat as before, 14D, but my seatmate must have been rebooked on a different flight, because the seat by the window was empty. I could not believe my good fortune. Could this be the reward for my exemplary behavior in the face of the crisis we'd all just experienced? A seat for me, and one for Jesus. It couldn't get better than that.

I was imagining how wonderful this flight would be. Too tired to keep reading, I decided I would simply nap and gaze out the window at the cloud formations above. It would be peaceful, I reasoned. Just me, with Jesus sitting there in the empty seat next to me.

That's when Max and his mom appeared. It was clear this experience had taken the wind out of their sails. Mom had that look in her eyes. The one that says, "I have used up every last bit of cool I can muster. The goal on this flight is to make it through without poking someone in the eye with the coffee stirrers on that little snack cart the flight attendants roll down the aisle." I'm guessing that's what she was thinking. I can't be sure.

When Mom and Max reached their aisle seat, one row ahead and across from me, Max's mom tried to get him to climb up in the seat while she loaded their bags in the overhead compartment. Max wasn't having it, though. He laid his little body out, right in the middle of the aisle, informing us all in no uncertain terms that sitting in an airplane seat for another hour or two was no longer on his agenda.

On the inside, I normally want to be compassionate and strong and helpful and kind. I want to come to your rescue when the going gets tough. But I know myself, and knowing oneself is often the biggest obstacle.

I keep track of all the details on my mental list of checks and balances. Give me a quiet moment in the middle of the night and I begin to recount in my head all the ways I've

31

missed the mark, the many times I've fallen short, the multiple missteps I've taken along the way. I relive all the little ways I've failed. The list is endless, I tell you. Endless!

Before I know it, I am throwing back the covers on our Tempur-Pedic mattress, kicking my feet into the air, and gasping for breath.

Oftentimes, in the middle of the night, it's the details of moments like this one on the airplane with Max and his mom that run through my mind. Because while I want to believe I'm compassionate and strong and helpful and kind, I also know that sometimes I'm only as good as the me I was on that plane a few months ago. And sometimes even that is a stretch.

That day, sitting on that second airplane, I looked at Max and his mom, struggling to keep her composure, and then I looked at the empty seat next to me. I watched Max's mom peel his body from the floor, her hair falling into her eyes, Max's face as red as Nebraska on a Saturday afternoon during football season, and I looked at the empty seat next to me. I watched Max's mom as she lowered herself into the aisle seat, buckled her seat belt around her waist, and pulled Max close onto her lap. I watched Max arch his back in protest, I saw the look of defeat on his mom's face, and I didn't offer to switch seats with her.

It would have been an easy gesture. Such a little thing. Just lean over, tap her on her shoulder, and let her and Max stretch out in 14D and 14E while I moved over to 13C. But that's not what I did. I shifted in my seat just a bit so I couldn't make eye contact with anyone else on the plane. Not the flight attendants who looked at me as they passed by, not the person in the opposite aisle seat one row behind me, and certainly not Max as he wailed in protest at having to sit down and be still until the plane could take off.

I left my book in my purse.

I imagined Jesus vacating the seat next to me. Leaving it empty for real.

We flew the entire flight—from Philadelphia to Detroit—with me holding on selfishly to two seats and Max and his exhausted mom sharing a seat just an aisle away. If this is the story of the Good Samaritan (see Luke 10:30–37), we all know which characters I was that day.

And let's be honest: not just that day.

At the very core of who I am sits the rabbi, the religious leader, the church member rushing by the person in need because I have "spiritual things" to attend to. I convince myself my spirituality is my status symbol, like a designer purse or a pair of tall boots or a fancy car with leather upholstery and a sunroof. But each night, it's as if I wash the whole thing down the drain, along with my mascara and my MAC foundation.

I've been listening to people tell the story of the Good Samaritan for as long as I can remember. It's a beautiful story, and it's easy to pick out the hero in the story. "In the story of the Good Samaritan, who is the good guy?" Wouldn't that be a great question on the latest version of those college entrance exams? That afternoon, one aisle seat removed from Max and his mom, the good guy on the plane was not me.

One day a few weeks after I slinked off that airplane and resumed life as usual in my hometown, I found myself riding my bike on the trails. It was one of those days when summer elbows her way back into fall, not willing to go down without a fight. These are the best kinds of days. Acorns crunched beneath the tires of my bike and one or two leaves fell to the ground as I rolled past. My tires carried me for miles and miles, and the one thing that kept churning in my mind was that story of the Good Samaritan in Luke 10.

The rabbi, the priest, the Samaritan. All the characters ran through my mind. In my imagination, I held them up to myself and made comparisons. In different moments and on different occasions, I've been like each one of them. I have rushed past, averting my gaze when I've seen someone in need, hurrying to get to my destination. I have crossed to the other side of the road in a weak and pitiful attempt at avoiding confrontation, or getting my hands dirty, or investing time where I hadn't intended to. I have let my schedule dictate my compassion. I have measured *agape* in shallow bowls of comfort and convenience.

But I have also been the good guy. Some days I do get it right. Some days I let loose of my agenda and my hurried chasing after glittery things, and I actually get it right. I think it's okay to admit that. Some days I miss the mark completely, and other days are stellar. It's just behavior. It's not who I am.

I get tripped up when I start identifying myself by what I do or don't do. Those things have nothing to do with grace (see Rom. 11:6).

I'd be lost without grace.

I'm not talking about the grace I have witnessed on stages in New York, when my mom used to take me to see the Alvin Ailey dancers and then wait in the alley with me for a glimpse of willowy limbs and hair pulled tight into buns atop the crowns of the ballet dancers' heads. That kind of grace is beautiful. But the grace of God is even more beautiful than that.

I believe Anne Lamott is on to something when she says, "I do not at all understand the mystery of grace—only that it meets us where we are but does not leave us where it found us."[1] Could it be that the biggest obstacle to receiving grace is refusing to admit our deep and aching need for it?

At some point on the journey, each of us will realize we'd be lost without grace, and we realize it before we ever have the words to say what it is that grace really means. Do we ever really find the words?

The rabbi, the priest, the Samaritan. I am all of these. I can be all of these. I can act like any of them. It all depends, doesn't it?

On the bike trail that afternoon, I passed beneath the low branches of a glorious tree whose green leaves skittered in the breeze and revealed to me a glimpse of golden light hiding in the foliage. I wondered just how long we'd have before the air turned crisp and I'd have to trade my sandals, shorts, and tank tops for warmer clothes. It was when I shifted gears and slowed things down on the bike trail that I remembered one more character in the story of the Good Samaritan in Luke 10.

When Jesus told that story, introducing us all to the renowned Good Samaritan, Jesus was answering a question posed by a man the Bible calls "an expert in the law" (v. 25 NIV). The man asked Jesus how he might inherit eternal life. Looking for a peace prize–worthy list of one hundred ways to guarantee eternal life, this expert asked Jesus straight up, "What do I need to *do* to inherit eternal life?" (v. 25, emphasis added).

Naturally, Jesus answered the question with a question. "Well," Jesus answered, "what does the Law say?" (see v. 26).

Of course, when Jesus and this expert were having their conversation, no one had a copy of the Bible in his or her back pocket, and there was no internet to turn to for quick and easy access to the books of the Law. The Law Jesus referred to was what we now consider the first five books of the Old Testament, or the Torah. The Torah contained 613 laws for the nation of Israel to follow. These laws were designed to set Israel apart so other nations would look at them and the way they lived their lives from one day to the next, and the people of those other nations would be able to say about the Israelites, "Oh yeah, those Israelites? Well, they're a bit different. They act like that because of the God they follow."

Did you see that part about there being 613 laws? That is a lot of laws, and being "an expert in the law," the guy asking the questions knew every last detail about every single one of those 613 laws. When Jesus asked him what he thought the Law had to say in answer to his question about inheriting eternal life, the expert reached into his vast storehouse of knowledge and whittled down all those laws to these two points: love God with everything I am, and love my neighbor as if he were me (see v. 27).

"Bingo!" Jesus said. (I'm paraphrasing.)

The expert, however, wasn't satisfied. He pressed Jesus a bit further, the way our children press us for five more minutes before bedtime, one more cookie, one more ride on the roller coaster of life. "But who, exactly, is my neighbor?" the expert asked (see v. 29).

That's when Jesus told the story, beginning with, "There was this guy headed on a trip from Jerusalem to Jericho, when out of the blue, some robbers jumped him, stripped him, beat him, and left him for dead . . ." (see v. 30).

I usually blow right past that part. I completely forget about this man on the side of the road, his body naked and broken and bloody, limbs jutting out from his torso at weird angles, his eyes rolled back in his head, his chest heaving as he gasps for breath. I rush ahead, trying to figure out how the guy from Samaria tapped into this grace described by Anne Lamott and wanting to be sure I can count myself good like him.

Good. Like him. I don't want to miss the mark. I don't want to fall short. I want to be like the Samaritan. I want to show up in Jesus's stories as an example of how one *should* behave.

But while riding my bike on the trail that day, I realized I'd skipped right over the poor guy left for dead on the side of the road. So, in my mind, I backed things up and took a good look at him. If I just throw a glance his way on my way to my next appointment, I might think he simply laid himself down on the side of the road to take a nap. If I hurry past him, I don't recognize his pain. If I avert my gaze, I miss the part about him being naked and broken and thirsty and all alone.

I studied the brokenness, with everything exposed and bleeding out. I took in the rattled breath and matted hair and desperation. I studied the vacant eyes and the parted lips, all cracked and swollen in the sun, and I could hear the vultures circling overhead. Can you see it too?

When I was a little girl, my grandfather—my mom's father—told me once that if I ever saw a crowd of people gathering around the scene of an accident, I should go the other way. My grandfather was trying to protect me. You never know what you might see in the center of that crowd with the wail of sirens piercing the air and ambulance lights flashing. It might be something you couldn't unsee, no matter how hard you tried.

One afternoon just about a year ago, I was a passenger in a vehicle on a California highway. The traffic ahead slowed suddenly, and I could see what appeared to be a puff of smoke mushroom above us on the road. Now, I believe that puff of smoke, lifting itself into the air, may have been the burning of rubber and brakes as one driver tried desperately to stop and avoid what by then was an inevitable tragedy. For a few minutes, traffic inched along, pressing into one lane, making way and slowly moving forward. I gripped the handle on the door of the car and squeezed hard as it became evident we were rolling up on the scene of a serious accident. Cars sat at angles to the road, and two or three young gentlemen were walking on the shoulder of the road with horrified looks on their faces. I remember thinking that one guy should sit down and apply pressure to the gash on his forehead. Blood flowed from the wound into his eyes, but the young man didn't seem to notice. His friend, walking on the shoulder with him, lifted both hands to his own head, and I followed his terrified gaze and instantly remembered my grandfather's advice.

On the shoulder, at least a hundred yards from the nearest stopped and battered vehicle, lay the figure of a young man. If he'd been lying anywhere else, I might have thought he was taking a nap. But he was on the asphalt, with his left cheek pressed into the gravel on the road. He didn't move. He didn't inhale. He didn't move his hand toward his nose to brush away a fly. He wore cream-colored denim pants and a shirt with stripes, and I never saw him move.

My grandfather was right. I don't think that's a scene I will ever forget. Sitting in the passenger seat, I reached for my cell phone and dialed 911. "There's been an accident," I said, my voice barely whispering its way into the device I held next to my ear. "We're on our way," the person on the other end said back to me.

Yes, these are the scenes most people would rush past if they could. And what I realize is that in the story of the Good Samaritan, this person on the side of the road, stripped and beaten and left for dead, looks an awful lot like me, desperate to hear the sound of sirens approaching from the distance. Hoping against hope that help is on the way. Suddenly, the rabbi and the religious leader and the compassionate man from Samaria are not my only options in the story. Suddenly, I realize I'm a lot like the man on the side of the road.

Beaten and left for dead. Wildly in need of help.

It's how I feel in those middle-of-the-night moments when I kick the covers off and gasp for oxygen to fill my lungs. I slide myself to the edge of the mattress and reach for the hardwoods with the big toe of my right foot. I try not to wake my husband as I grope my way to the bathroom, where I lean on the edge of the sink and try not to replay events like Max and his mom on the plane. I am broken, and I can hear the vultures circling overhead.

"You're a mess. Look at you, all naked and exposed. You're bleeding all over everything, and you've been violated, and you are gross. Just gross." If I'm not careful, I might believe those words. I *have* believed those words. I have wrapped them around me like a beautiful scarf and worn them as my identity. I have let them settle in my heart, and I have drawn the shades, and I have felt the grime of road dust way back in my wisdom teeth.

Just gross.

"God doesn't want you. God can't even work with you. You are beyond help. Who are you to think you can make a difference? Just keep to your routine. Stay in your lane. Stop looking up."

Have you heard it too? It's enough to make you want to schedule an appointment with God so that you can turn in your resignation. What was it that ever made you think God would want to hang around with you?

Lying on the side of the road to Jericho, broken and beaten and left for dead, the man in the Bible story may have watched the rabbi and the religious leader pass by on the other side of the road. He couldn't blame them, really. He was a mess, and he imagined he looked as if all the life had oozed right out of him and stained the ground right where he lay. What a wretched embarrassment he must be. Beyond help. Past the point of no return. Desperately lost. If he could kick the covers off and take a gulp of air, he would. In the middle of the night, I lean on the bathroom sink and I feel like his twin.

But there are footsteps in the dust. I hear the crunch of dirt and stone beneath the soles of sandals, and I realize those footsteps are headed in my direction. And when I squint to peer through all the grossness, I find myself face-to-face with the only real Good Guy there ever was, and I want to say to him, "Don't touch me. You'll get yourself all dirty. Let me cover myself up first with this scarf I have. I'm gross. Can't you see? I am gross."

But he's persistent. He is not content to leave me as he's found me. And I can hardly believe it without cringing. "Me? You are here for me?" I want to ask.

God loves you and me, just the way we are—prone to wander and all the rest. And we're the only ones who put a question mark at the end of those two letters: m and e. "Me?" we say to God, an index finger pointed to our own chest, unconvinced he can find anything redeemable in there. In here. Don't be fooled. You are never too far gone. Your abandonment, abortion, addiction, adultery, aggression, anger, angst, anxiety, attitude, avoidance—none of it is going to cause God to walk past without looking in your direction. And those are just the *A*s. Paul says in Romans 8:35, "Do you think anyone is going to be able to drive a wedge between us and Christ's love for us? There is no way! Not trouble, not hard times, not hatred, not hunger, not homelessness, not bullying threats, not backstabbing, not even the worst sins listed in Scripture."

Not even the worst sins listed in Scripture. What is it that you have done? What is the tape you keep playing in your head? What is it that has left you undone and feeling unworthy of the love of God? Run your own list, and check it twice. Then hold that list up against Romans 8 and see for yourself. Nothing can get between you and God's deep, true, real, and sincere love for you. It could just as easily be you there—beaten and broken and left in the dust. Dead to the world. And with those footsteps headed in your direction.

"You're not gross," he says. "And besides"—now he's sliding his hand beneath your head—"I can fix this," he says, because he's also not one to leave you the way he found you. And now the question sounds like this: "Will you let me?"

You're not gross. Maybe a little battered and bruised. Or, if we're honest, you might actually have your toes curled over the edge of that cliff and be one gust of wind short of throwing in the towel. But you're not gross. Do you hear me? *You are not gross.* You are not beyond God's reach, no matter how far off track you may have wandered. God has designs on you. Remember? He is not waiting for someone else. God is waiting for you. God wants you. God loves you exactly the way you are right this very minute.

Yes. You.

In the bathroom, leaning on the edge of the sink, with my husband asleep on his side of our bed, there is only one word I can muster. It rises up from my dusty, swirling thoughts and lets me breathe. "Jesus." I reach for the light switch on the bathroom wall, and the room goes dark, and I'm good with that, because the Light scatters the darkness—every single time. I missed the mark with Max and his mom. There can be no mistaking that. There will be no going back to fix it. No making it right. And tomorrow I will miss the mark again. But the darkness doesn't stand a chance.

So I shuffle—softly now—across the hardwoods, and I climb back into bed and rest my head on the pillow. I can hear the question in my ears: "Will you let me?"

I'm that guy on the side of the road, parting my cracked and swollen lips to receive the wine, spilled for me. And for you. Will you let him?

★ ★ ★ ★ ★ *2* ★ ★ ★ ★ ★

The Cherry Tree Has Got to Go

The gospel does not make sense unless you have the
heart to enter into your own shame.

Dan Allender

When she was a senior in high school, my sister spent her
spring break in Mexico. Then when she graduated from college, my sister moved to Mexico, where she lived and worked
for five years. Eventually, an amazing gentleman she knew
from college put a ring on her finger, and my sister moved
back to Virginia. But first, my sister fell in love with Mexico.

I envied her.

I was a new mom, simply trying to make my way from
breakfast to bedtime without a trip to the emergency room

and with limited encounters with the time-out chair—for my children and for me. Some seasons of life are like that, with each moment marking a small victory, primarily because we survived it. In these seasons, the thoughts we had of making a difference, of leaving our mark, of pointing people to God, begin to slip through our fingers, and if we're not careful, we might begin thinking our lives aren't really making a difference at all. Stories of my sister's life in Mexico seemed so grand compared to my small existence in my nondescript, three-bedroom home. I began wondering if the grass really might be greener on the other side of the border.

My sister, Karen, is four years and eleven months younger than me. To the day. We didn't hang out together much when we were growing up. Our interests and ages kept us in different circles. When she was five, I was ten. When she was ten, I was fifteen. Our worlds didn't jive back then. Before I knew it, I had gotten married and moved out, and my sister was still in high school.

Our family lived on a cul-de-sac when my sister and I were little. Our modest wooden house was painted yellow with brown shutters. A small Japanese maple tree grew right by the front steps. If I close my eyes, I can transport myself right back to that yellow Cape Cod house on Sycamore Avenue, its dormered windows welcoming me with eyes wide open. I remember the address. I remember my phone number from way back then, when everyone had a landline (some people, whom I envied, even had a party line) and we had what must have been the longest beige telephone cord in recorded history.

Some days, I'd run through the house and find myself wrapped up in the spiraling phone cord my mom stretched from the telephone on one side of the kitchen all the way over to the portable dishwasher on the other side. And when I say *all the way over*, I probably mean something like ten feet, a distance that looks completely different when you're nine years old.

On the outside of our yellow house on Sycamore Avenue, green and white variegated hosta plants grew low around the foundation. Late in summer, brave shoots seemed to levitate from the green leaves that hugged the ground. It always took me by surprise. One day I'd be wearing my bathing suit in the front yard, running through the sprinkler with my friends from the neighborhood, and the next day I'd stand in that very same spot, marveling at the lavender flowers blossoming from the tips of those green shoots suddenly standing tall beneath the living room window, keeping watch over our yard.

I fell in love with cherries in the side yard of that yellow Cape Cod house. Just outside the living room window and next to the red brick chimney grew a fruit-bearing cherry tree. I learned to spot a perfect cherry from a mile away. Dark burgundy skin (the same color, I'd later discover, of a really wonderful Merlot), no dimples or bruises, firm between my thumb and index finger.

I'd dangle a cherry from its stem, tilt my head back, and lower the fruit into my mouth. My front teeth closed to separate the orb from its stem, and then I'd let the fruit rest on my tongue. *Patience*, I seemed to say to myself, although it would be a long time before I understood the meaning of the word. The cherry rested on my tongue for as long as I could stand it—about one-seventeenth of one second—then I'd roll it over between my molars and slowly bite down, stopping at the pit and releasing an explosion of sweetness. Sometimes the wine-colored essence trickled from the corner of my mouth. It all happened much more quickly than I've described. Anyone watching me from the living room window might think I was simply shoving in one cherry after another after another, until my belly could no longer stand it. In my mind, there were hundreds of cherries, but *scores* is probably a better estimation.

One day I learned the cherry tree had to go. My dad had looked in the Yellow Pages, or he had talked with a neighbor or to the guy at the gas station around the corner and down the street, and hired someone who would come to our home and chop that tree down to the ground with a chain saw or an ax or some other instrument of destruction. Then, as if to put an exclamation mark at the end of the whole thing, this person would grind out the roots of that tree so that it would never grow, never again offer fruit for a lazy summer afternoon.

I was devastated.

I may have cried.

I remember standing beside that cherry tree after learning of its fate. I remember the smooth, dark bark on the outside of the trunk, its texture like linen and silk. I remember wondering what the tree had done wrong.

"Carpenter ants," my dad told me.

"Carpenter ants?" I asked.

My dad led me around to the back of the house, to the screened-in porch just off the kitchen. The screened-in porch was my mother's favorite thing. We ate dinner out there, played dress-up, and bounced my baby sister in her swing. We read stories and told stories and sat quietly to wait for a breeze. Grown-ups took naps out there on the screened-in porch, and we watched lightning bugs glow in Mason jars before releasing them again into the night.

Now, the fate of the cherry tree foremost on my mind, I stood next to my dad, who had somehow managed to wrestle a long two-by-four from where it had served some role as part of our screened-in porch. The board had been wrenched free, and now it was at my feet in the dark, loamy soil, and my dad encouraged me to look closer. "Carpenter ants," he said again.

I still didn't get it, and my face must have betrayed my confusion, because my dad leaned closer—forever patient with me—and pointed to what looked like tunnels that had been carved out of the wood. From the outside, nailed up as part of our screened-in porch, that two-by-four looked solid and appeared to offer a firm foundation. But here, detached from its place as part of the porch and turned over with its decimated underbelly exposed for all the world to see, I could tell this two-by-four was a farce and that it had been ruined from the inside out. "The cherry tree has carpenter ants, and they've gotten into the house."

Suddenly, I understood. The cherry tree had to go. I may have loved cherries, but I loved my life with my family in this little wooden yellow house on the cul-de-sac way more than I loved cherries.

I loved every evening when my dad came home from work with his dry cleaning slung over his shoulder. I loved the way my mom let me sit on the kitchen counter while she mixed pound cake batter with the hand mixer and then let me lick the beaters and the spoon and the bowl. I loved when my sister and I lay in our twin beds beneath the pitched roof, drifting to sleep to the sounds of crickets outside and my mother playing the piano or running the vacuum cleaner in the living room below. I loved sitting at the dinner table in our kitchen, my feet wrapped around the rungs of the chair, all four of us holding hands while my dad said grace. I loved the screened-in back porch.

If carpenter ants were threatening to destroy all that, then they had to go.

Having done the kind of detective work homeowners often do, my dad discovered the home base of our personal carpenter ants was inside the cherry tree. He walked me back around to the tree, and we stood there together while he helped me to see what not too long before had been hidden to me. Tiny holes, the same diameter as those tunnels in the two-by-four my dad had pulled from the house, speckled the bark of the tree. And when I focused my eyes up a little bit higher, I could see those carpenter ants with their three-sectioned bodies marching single-file along one of the branches overhead. *How, I wondered to myself, could something so terrible be hidden in such a beautiful tree?*

Not long after I watched those carpenter ants marching around on the branch of the cherry tree, a man came to our house and destroyed that tree—ants and all. The man packed up his gear and left our yard, and I remember standing near where the tree once stood. One thick branch lay on the ground, its bark a beautiful combination of linen and silk. But I could have crushed that branch to smithereens with the child-sized Buster Brown T-strap loafers I wore on my little feet, because that branch was nearly hollow—just a shell of itself. Those pesky carpenter ants had devoured the branch's core.

And so, it is cherries that sometimes help me remember God. Or rather, to remember that God's goodness has an enemy.

I probably believed in the devil before I believed in God. I don't mean I believed *in following* the devil. What I mean to say is, I knew there is evil in the world. I knew fear before I knew freedom.

At night, in my childhood bed, I'd sometimes tuck the covers around my neck and under my chin, my eyes squeezed tightly against the dark. Always, always, every single night, my bedtime prayer was, "Dear God, please don't let me be scared. Please don't let anything happen that I think is scary, and please don't let me think of anything I think is scary. Amen." I was trying to cover all the bases. I had a feeling that just because I thought something was scary didn't mean God did. I wanted to be sure God and I were on the same page and that he was prepared to protect me from all of it. I couldn't be sure God wasn't the same as everyone else, looking at me with a wry smile and saying, "Oh, that? Now, *that's* nothing to be afraid of."

I was a full-grown adult with two children of my own before I finally realized this simple truth: the devil is a liar. I had to hear it over and over again before it finally stuck. The first time I heard it was from a preacher who stood draped in black robes, his hands holding either side of the wooden pulpit in front of him. "The devil is a liar," he said in a voice that sounded like thunderclouds, "and when he speaks, he speaks his native tongue." I thought the words sounded fancy, but I wasn't ready to trust them yet. I went home and prayed my please-don't-let-me-be-scared prayer. Later, I read more about what that preacher was trying to tell us. The story unfolds in John chapter 8.

It seems Jesus was getting an early start on the day. And so was one particular woman who, the Bible says, was "caught in the act of adultery" (v. 3 NLT). (Admittedly, we could spend hours right there. How were they able to "catch" her?

49

If she was committing adultery, where was her partner in this crime? Who did these people think they were?)

Jesus had been traveling around, preaching about hope and good things, and oddly, he was making the religious people nervous. They were starting to wonder who this guy was and how his presence would impact them. So they started testing Jesus and trying to catch *him* in some slipup along the way. The best they could do was to spy on a woman, snatch her from her private world, and drag her into the synagogue.

Can you imagine? Being caught *in the act of* adultery didn't mean being caught having a drink at the pub in the next town over. No. It meant sex. A gang of religious men tracked her down and burst in on her. On them. Because there had to be someone else there, right?

We don't know if they gave her time to stop in the bathroom or to wrap the sheets around her. These religious men grabbed her, and wrestling her like a bag of garbage being taken to the curb, they burst into the temple courts, hurled themselves down the aisle, and cast this woman at the feet of Jesus, who was teaching in the synagogue about the kingdom of God.

"Teacher," the men must have sneered at Jesus, wiping the backs of their hands across their twisted mouths or licking their lips while their chests heaved up and down with the pride of their latest conquest. "What about this woman? What about *her*?"—as if the word required one to spit in the dirt after saying it and then step on the saliva and grind it into the dirt beneath a leather sandal. Grind *her* into the dirt. Maybe the person with whom she'd been caught was standing in the crowd too, ready to pick up a stone at the word *go*.

You know the words: *Slut. Whore. Sinner. Fast. Loose. Easy.* And worse.

50

The excuses: She was asking for it. What did she expect? Look how she dresses! Everyone knows that's the way she is. She's always been that way.

Anyone who's lived a few years has had someone try to tell them they just don't measure up. Never have. Never will. Sometimes we're the ones who start the rumor against ourselves. *Life sure looks better on her side of the fence,* we say to ourselves as we go through the motions of Life as We Know It. Trace those words to their root, and every single time, you'll find the Liar-in-Chief, marching around on a branch like a three-sectioned carpenter ant, practically undetected and eating away from the inside out. He is clear about his job description; it's the job description Jesus reminds us of in John 10:10: "A thief is only there to steal and kill and destroy."

Our enemy is well aware of his role, and he is hell-bent on fulfilling it.

Once, when my sister and I were young—four and nine, I imagine—I lost my sister. One day in that little yellow house where I lived with my family, I asked my mom if I could go to my friend's house to play. "Take your sister," my mother said.

"Take my sister?" I wanted to whine. Ugh.

My friend lived on the corner, her house facing the street to which Sycamore Avenue connected. To visit this particular friend, we'd walk down the street and to my friend's driveway, which emptied onto Sycamore Avenue. From there we entered the house through the back door, avoiding altogether the busy cross street.

That afternoon I walked with my friends, talking about all the serious things nine-year-olds discuss. My sister lagged behind, and every now and then I'd turn around or glance over my shoulder to make sure she was still there.

51

And then I forgot all about her.

Back at home, my mom says, she was on the telephone in the kitchen, the long, beige telephone cord stretched so she could see the front door. The door opened and in walked my sister, followed by a man we'd never seen before and never saw again.

"Is this your daughter?" the man asked my mom. Then, exasperated, "She was in the street!" My very own heart just dropped to the pit of my stomach as I typed those words. My mom says that man gave her a look of disgust, then turned on his heels, made a sound of contempt, and walked out the door.

In that moment, my mom told me, she felt judged and convicted of being a neglectful and uncaring mother. Oh, how it must have looked to that man! My mom, relaxed and cozy, chatting it up on the kitchen phone while her preschool-aged daughter wandered near the busy street. Even now, more than forty years later, my mom and I both shudder when we recount the tale, and then my mother sighs and says, "God looks after fools and babies."

It's a testament to my mother that she never scolded me for losing my sister. She didn't throw me under the bus. I only know the story because she eventually told it to me, but never in way that shamed me, and never in a way that made me want to wrap a sheet around myself, the way the woman in John chapter 8 may have wanted to. If I could see that man looking disgustedly at my mom, I would put my little hands on my tiny nine-year-old hips and say to him, "Liar, liar! My mom is not neglectful! She is not uncaring! My mom would move heaven and earth for me!"

But I am not nine, and I've learned about patience and about grace. And I am so very grateful to that man for bringing my sister home.

It is also a testament to my mom that she didn't let that man's impression of her define her. She learned from that experience, she says. But she also says she was clear she'd had no ill intent; she is simply human. And humans make mistakes.

I don't know that man, but I believe he was afraid. I believe that when he saw a little girl playing in a busy street, it terrified him, just as it still terrifies and threatens to shame me when I think about it for too long. I think that man felt a lot like those religious people back in the day: afraid. They worried the appearance of Jesus on the scene was upsetting their religious apple cart. So they tracked down a woman and brought her to Jesus, sounds of contempt filling the air. Voicing their own please-don't-let-me-be-scared prayers, they spoke the words about how she was unworthy. Unfit for anything but stoning. And Jesus called them out, inviting the perfect one among them to throw the very first stone (see John 8:7).

No one. None perfect. Except, of course, for Jesus, who doodled in the sand instead of picking up even a single stone. "Next time," Jesus said to the woman, "make a different choice" (see v. 11). He knew who she really was. He knew what she was capable of. And Jesus knew a lie when he saw it. Jesus knew her sin was not too big for the gift of grace, not too scathing for an offering of mercy. Her sin—like yours, and like mine—was not enough to render her not enough. God's incomprehensible love for us looks right past our mess-ups, our mishaps, our mistakes and extends a hand of forgiveness before we even know we need it.

At the very end of what must have been a very long day, a day he'd spent patiently trying to share a little good news with the religious people gathered in the temple, Jesus looked over the crowd, their quizzical faces turned in his direction, and said

53

something that sounded like this: "You know why you don't get this? You've been listening to lies for far too long. Somehow, you've been convinced the lie is the truth. But let me tell you something. When you're listening to lies, you're listening to the devil. It's the only language he knows" (see John 8:42–44).

Lying, for the devil, is not a second language he's trying to master. Lying never gets old to him. He is not bilingual. He knows no other language. When he speaks, he speaks his native tongue, and while it may look like linen and silk on the outside, on the inside it has been eaten away—decimated—just like that cherry tree.

The language of the enemy is insipid and vile and vacant and void. It will kill your dreams, it will drench you in shame, it will steal your hope, and it will destroy your peace. It will keep you from believing the truth about yourself. It will keep you looking down at the ground. It will make you think everyone else is better off than you. It will keep you cowering in a filthy old bedsheet, expecting a torrent of stones to rain down on the crown of your head.

The lies we tell ourselves—I'm too old, too young, too big, too small, too dark, too light, too new at this whole thing, too messed up, too busy, too bored, too boring, too comfortable, too sinful, too far gone—stand like sentinels between us and the callings God has uniquely designed for us. Like persistent carpenter ants, they destroy our dreams from the inside out, leaving us hollow and doubting we will ever do anything that makes any difference at all. Don't build your life on that kind of foundation.

The day I lost my sister, my mother could have wrapped up that experience in lovely paper, tied it with a velvet bow, and attached an elegant letterpress tag to the package with

54

my name on it. She could have insisted I carry the weight of that moment in a package of shame and transgression. I could have spent my childhood believing I'd done the unforgivable. But my mom wasn't having that. She refused to saddle me with a language of lies.

Jesus has done the same on a much grander scale. Refusing to let us be weighed down by the tangled web of deceit, Jesus took the blame. He walked up to the Liar-in-Chief, took your shame, and wrote his own name on it. Whatever it is—that thing you think makes you too filthy—Christ has already paid the price for it. The punishment has been rendered, and we have been set free. God is not the one who tricks us into thinking we're so far gone there is no way back. He doesn't measure the significance of our lives by the highlights alone. If you've been thinking you're past the point of no return, take a good look at that message and consider the source.

There is a difference between conviction and condemnation. You've probably experienced it. Conviction comes from the Holy Spirit, and it is gentle and loving and free from feelings of guilt and shame. Conviction is the hand of a loving Father, not raised against us in opposition but gently pointing to the path we somehow wandered from and shining a light to lead us back toward him.

Condemnation, however, follows on the heels of a string of empty lies, and it saddles us with guilt and shame and renders us paralyzed, with our borders tightly drawn and the sheets pulled snug beneath our chins, waiting for the first stone to fall. Condemnation convinces us we'll never measure up and that all would be well if we could only live so-and-so's life. Condemnation slithers in and makes us look at the life we've been given, the place where we live, the people under our roof and across from us at the dining room table and wish they were all something or somebody different. Condemnation takes us outside to stand beneath that cherry tree. It points at the tree, and instead of deciding the tree needs to come down, we decide to pack our bags and move out of that little yellow house on the cul-de-sac, forfeiting the screened-in porch and the hands held around the table and the saying of grace. Condemnation is the work of the enemy, and it is the direct translation of all his empty accusations.

Don't be fooled by the linen and the satin. Don't be taken in by the destructive voice of the enemy of your soul. All of us have missed the mark. Each one of us has wandered off the path. We've known shame and we are acquainted with sin. That is the truth about humanity, and the enemy would have us believe we are without hope.

But Jesus tells the truth about our situation. Jesus tells a different story. Jesus tells a story of a God who loves us and will never give up on us. God doesn't see our sin as the end of the road or the last chapter in the book. He is not deterred by the humdrum seasons of life where everyone else seems to have it going on and all we've got is diapers and no new recipes for chicken breasts. The life you are living is worth it. The future God has for you is worth fighting for. He calls us to faithfulness in both the miraculous and the mundane. The memories you are making are bigger than you know, and they will sustain you when you least expect it.

The cherry tree has got to go, and you can crush it with your Buster Browns. You can crush it with the name of Jesus.

★ ★ ★ ★ ★ ★ *3* ★ ★ ★ ★ ★ ★

The Opposite of Fear

Don't be afraid, I've redeemed you.
  I've called your name. You're mine.
When you're in over your head, I'll be there with you.
  When you're in rough waters, you will not go
  down.
When you're between a rock and a hard place,
  it won't be a dead end—
Because I am GOD, your personal God,
  The Holy of Israel, your Savior.

Isaiah 43:2–3

One of the trickiest things about fear is that it doesn't disappear simply because you've decided you want to do something risky or something that takes you outside your comfort zone. Fear feels bigger than your greatest ambitions and more powerful than your deepest longings. It dwarfs your dreams and saps the wonder from your imagination. And so there you stand, right at the threshold where faith and fear meet, because some of the most exciting, enriching, and life-changing adventures to which God invites you begin with a single step outside the places where you feel most safe. You stand there with your stomach in knots, your heart doing backflips against your ribs, your breath coming in short pinches, your right arm instinctively stretching out across the passenger seat. You've forgotten that fear doesn't disqualify you from the thing God is calling you to.

When I turned fifty, my husband took me to Hawaii. My sister, cheering us on from her home in Virginia, named our trip Hawaii Five-Oh, and the name stuck. This was our third trip to Hawaii, our first to Maui. My husband has a strategy. Sometimes when we're standing in the kitchen, or driving down the road, or sitting in the backyard with a fire in the fire pit, he'll look at me and say, "I'm going to keep taking you to Hawaii until you decide you want to move there." He loves Hawaii. So I suffer through. (That's a joke. There is no suffering involved.)

We went to Maui for the snorkeling.

The ocean captivates me. I am convinced I could stand on the shore for days without moving. All of nature moves me—all of it in different ways. But the ocean stirs my soul in ways I can't describe. I am mesmerized when I consider what it must have been like when God spoke and separated the sky from the ocean and raised up mountains and carved out ravines and crevasses and then filled the sky with stars and planets and galaxies and constellations while he stocked the seas with fish and coral and anemones and whales and seahorses. Seahorses!

It takes my breath away.

"It's like outer space," Harry told me when we were in Maui and I was holding back tears, trying to put my feelings into words. And maybe it is like outer space. The ocean stretches itself out across the miles and practically shouts to me in sacred whispers that God is bigger than my mind will ever know this side of heaven.

I am not a good swimmer. Despite (or perhaps because of) my deep emotional attachment to the wonder of the ocean, I am well aware of its great power to demolish me with one shift of its majestic current. I am tentative on my approach and slow to commit. I like the ground beneath my feet, the water no higher than my ears. I don't mess with the waves.

My first experience with snorkeling had been on our honeymoon in the Bahamas where I had naively donned the mask and fins while wearing a cute little honeymoon-worthy, electric-blue bikini. In the Bahamas, I'd followed Harry's instructions and soon found myself entranced by sightings just beneath the surface of the water of fabulously designed fish, some of which matched my hot little bathing suit.

We had stayed out quite a while, and when I finally looked up, I realized (a) my feet no longer reached the bottom, and (b) I had drifted quite a distance from shore. And that, as they say, was all she wrote. I thought for sure I was going to die. On my honeymoon. In the Bahamas. What would Harry tell my parents?

I began to struggle, thrashing about in the water. Okay, I probably wasn't thrashing. It was probably more like frantic little slaps at the water, splashing spits of salty wetness into my own face. I thought I must have been a sight for my new husband who, I eventually realized, didn't even notice I was dying. All I could see was the back of him, floating along on the surface of the water with that darned snorkeling breathing tube thing poking up into the air.

So I started to swim for shore. But I wasn't sure I would make it. I didn't know enough about the buoyancy of salt water or the efficiency of the fins I was wearing to remain calm. Instead, I gasped and sputtered my way toward shallower water, hoping I could keep it together long enough to reach the place where I could finally touch bottom again.

Somewhere along the way, I heard Harry's voice behind me. "What happened?" he asked, and my look must have betrayed my fear. He took me by the arm and guided me safely to shore, where I crawled on the sand, gasping for air in my electric-blue bikini, and vowed to never do that again.

And yet we went to Maui for the snorkeling, which I imagined could be done in waist-deep water, my feet fixed firmly on the ground. The summer before our Maui trip, we'd been snorkeling in the Florida Keys, where a person can wade out for-what-seems-like-ever with the clear turquoise and emerald water never passing any higher than her waist. Snorkeling in the Florida Keys expeditiously wiped the memory of the Bahamas clear out of my mind.

We should plan a snorkeling trip, Harry and I decided on our way home from Florida. So when we returned to Nebraska, we contacted a travel agent and asked her to send us to a place where snorkeling was all the rage. My Panic in the Bahamas episode was the furthest thing from my mind, and so, for my fiftieth birthday, we booked a trip to Maui.

"Be careful out there," the concierge at our Maui hotel told us when we mentioned our snorkeling plans. "It drops off pretty quick."

I promise you, I tried not to let those words stick in my head.

"She has to say that," I thought to myself that first day I stood at the shore in Maui, snorkel gear in my hands. "They have to cover their bases. It can't be *that* bad."

This time I was wearing a snappy little one-piece suit. Harry had already been in the water, and as I balanced on my left leg and used my index finger to pull an orange-and-black fin over the heel of my right foot, he said, "They're right. It does drop off." He said it gently and with the same intention as a mother with her arm reaching out across the passenger seat. I tried to let it roll off my back. I shifted my weight and balanced on my right leg as I pulled the other fin over the heel of my left foot.

"Okay," I said. "Thanks." I don't know if I sounded fearful. But I was getting there.

"There are some pretty cool fish out there," Harry was saying. He pointed in an arc, and I continued the imaginary line to a point not too far out at all. Not even beyond the waves. I stood up straight and pulled the mask down over my face, flattening my hands against the glass to seal it shut to keep the water out.

"You ready?" he was asking, inching his way toward the sea.

"I'm just going to take my time," I said, realizing my feet had melded themselves to the sand. I didn't let on. I put my hands on my hips.

"Sure," Harry said. "You'll be fine. Take your time." There was hardly anyone on the beach and only a few people in the water. A few feet to my right, another couple waded into the ocean. I watched, holding my breath, as they approached the legendary drop-off.

"Are you getting in?" Harry asked me.

"I am," I said. "I just have to go at my own speed." I was terrified. What if I got swept out to sea? What if I got caught in the undertow? What if I sank straight to the bottom? What if my heart stopped beating somewhere out there?

"Here." He was standing waist-deep in the water, holding out his hand. I took a step forward. I took two steps. I took enough steps to reach out and grab his hand.

"Where's the drop-off?" I asked. But he had no idea what I said, because I had that stupid air tube thing in my mouth.

"Here's the drop-off," he said. He took one step, and just like that the water reached his shoulders. He still had my hand. My feet were still on the ground, the water just splashing at my waist. I screamed anyway. Short little screams that felt locked down in my throat. The couple who had waded in just before us turned sharply to look my way.

Harry stayed calm. He looked over at the couple and smiled, and he stepped back up from the drop-off, still holding my hand. I stopped screaming and retreated to dry ground. Taking off the fins and mask, I said, "I'll try again later." But we both knew I was just saying that.

We didn't mention it again for the next six days of our vacation. We swam in the pool. We woke up early in the morning and drove to watch the sunrise from the top of a sleeping volcano. We drove the winding road toward Hana and climbed on lava rocks. We saw the end of rainbows and we drank strawberry piña coladas. We ate dessert. We watched whales from the balcony of our hotel room. We ran together in the mornings and competed in a 5K at the Maui YMCA. I lounged on the beach while Harry drifted on the water and then came back to tell me about the fish he'd seen in the sea. We unwound and relaxed and found the groove we didn't even realize we had lost. Oh my goodness, it was fabulous.

On our last full day in Maui, I sat by the pool in a lounge chair while Harry swam in the ocean. My shoulders hung low and easy as I inhaled the ocean air with its exotic mix of sea spray, sunscreen, and saltiness. Palm branches slipped across each other in the breeze, and a bird swam low above the pool, the water reflecting blue on the feathers beneath his wings. Every now and then, I read a few lines from Barbara Brown Taylor's book *Learning to Walk in the Dark*. But mostly, I let my heart and my lungs do their thing.

"I got something for you," Harry said. He stood over me, the stunning azure sky a canvas behind him.

"You did?" I asked.

"I did," he said, holding up a gigantic yellow life preserver. It was the kind of life preserver the lifeguards on *Baywatch* use as they run across the sand in perfect form. But I am not a lifeguard, and this massive yellow contraption was not sexy.

"That's for me?" I asked.

"Yes. I got it for you so you can go snorkeling." Then he held up my snorkel fins and mask in his other hand. "Here," he said, reaching both hands out to me, "put 'em on."

I don't know why, but I sat up, swung my legs over the edge of my lounge chair, planted my feet on the pool deck, and stood up. I reached into my bag for sunscreen, flipped open the top, and squeezed a dollop into my palm. Rubbing the sunscreen into my arms and shoulders, I stepped into my sandals and then reached out to take the fins, the mask, and that massive yellow life preserver from my husband. "Let's go," I said.

We made our way past the sunbathers and the children riding through the pool perched on their fathers' backs. We sauntered past the sunglasses vendor and the massage cabana. We crossed the path from the pool area onto the sand, and we moved with purpose. Onlookers probably thought I did this every day. They probably figured I knew what I was doing—unless they happened to catch a glimpse of that oversized life preserver in my hand.

Standing in the sand, I stepped out of my sandals and once again balanced myself while I slipped those fins onto my feet. I pulled the mask down over my head, and then I clipped that big yellow banana of a life preserver around my waist. It was so big it dropped to my hips and hung there like a carnival game ring around the neck of a cola bottle.

Not sexy.

"You ready?" Harry asked me, holding out his hand.

"I'm just going to take my time," I said—a repeat of our first day on the beach. "You go ahead. I'm coming."

"You can't sink," Harry said to me. "Between the salt water, the fins, and that life preserver, you won't drown. It's impossible."

I can't tell you how I got myself into that water. I don't remember. I know I did it on my own, without Harry pulling me or forcing me. He's not like that. He is used to me. He knows me, he loves me, and I trust him.

But somehow I found myself facedown on the surface of the water, the sound of my breathing in my ears, my teeth and lips closed around that silly breathing tube thing, that atrocious yellow life preserver around my waist, and my hand in Harry's hand. It was breathtakingly beautiful. So beautiful that the memory makes me cry right now just telling you about it.

What I know is that I was afraid. In fact, every now and then, the idea that I was floating in an ocean that could possibly kill me would rise up like mercury on a thermometer, and I'd pop my head up out of the water to make sure I could still see land. I'd sputter and gasp, and Harry would say, "What happened?" I'd shake my head, Harry would smile, and we'd float again for a few minutes until I felt the need to pop my head up again and check to be sure we hadn't drifted to Norway.

Or I'd be floating along, looking down at the ocean's floor, and the current would shift the sand beneath me, sending a literal wave of panic across my spine, causing me to stop breathing and, as a result, pop my head out of the water once again.

Through all these moments of panic, Harry kept holding my hand, like a lifeline to sanity and calm. Slowly—oh, so slowly—I was able to get myself out of my head, and like stars that gradually come on the scene at twilight, the beauty of the world beneath the surface of the sea began to unfold before my eyes.

What are the words for something like this?

Hand in hand we swam, pointing out the beautiful corals and urchins and fabulously colored fish as they danced and darted and lolled about just below us. The colors! The shapes! The beauty! Oh, what a glorious thing I would have missed, sitting on the sidelines with my fins and mask and breathing tube tucked beneath my poolside lounge chair. What an adventure I'd have shunned, standing on the shore, handing over my life to the straight-arm of fear.

What magnificence—what glory to behold!

In my ears, my breath was easy, measured out in deep, deep sighs of contented satisfaction, and I felt Harry gently squeeze my hand. I looked over at him, both of us peering out from behind our masks, and he gave me the thumbs-up sign. *You're doing it*, he seemed to say.

The water held me gently, rocking me in comfortable assurance, and I was overwhelmed. My throat tightened, and I would have cried if I could have figured out how to cry and be facedown on the surface of the Pacific Ocean at the same time. And so I breathed, and I surrendered to the waters and the warm sun on my back and the glorious invention of that gigantic yellow life preserver. And the waters did not consume me.

I don't know how long we floated out there in the ocean, taking in the beauty of God's creativity. But I know I could have stayed there forever. When Harry motioned that we should head back to shore, I whispered a silent prayer of gratitude to God for getting me across the threshold of the drop-off and extending such an amazing invitation. Side by side now, our heads above the water, our arms making lazy figure eights just beneath the surface, our feet suspended beneath us in the water, Harry and I hung there in the ocean for a bit, and I tried to find the words to tell him just how beautiful it was.

"It's like outer space," he said, when I couldn't find the words without spilling tears into the veil of water that wrapped itself around me and held me up to God. Like worship.

"Thank you," I answered. And I meant so many things.

Our physical bodies are wired to warn us when we need to pay special attention so that we'll stay safe. That warning is something we call fear, and it is good and right and it serves us well. And that is just the point. Fear is designed to serve us. Not control us. Fear says, "Well, here's something new and a little bit risky. Have you paid attention to the risks? Do you have your yellow life preserver?"

A healthy response to fear is to give attention to it but not to surrender control. Do you need a yellow life preserver? Then by all means, get one. Do you need an accountant to help get your finances under control? Go for it. Do you need a counselor to help you work through some knots in a relationship? Make that phone call. Do you need to stop, look, and listen before you cross the street? No problem. One small step at a time.

Don't let fear keep you from crossing the threshold or stepping off the drop-off into what God has in store for you. Even if you've heard him wrong or if you've gotten your wires crossed, you will not be consumed. God will rescue you and set your feet on solid ground.

He is out there in the ocean, laughing loud and splashing around in the waves, inviting you to join the fun. But he is also standing closer than you'd ever imagine as your eyes scan the horizon where the sea and sky fall into each another. God is standing right there with you at the edge of the drop-off, holding out his hand to you, and he's practically bursting with the excitement of taking you with him. You can thank fear for reminding you to check your parachute to make sure it's packed correctly, and then you can leave fear right there on the threshold. It wouldn't come anyway. It's too afraid. But you? You can put your hand in God's hand, take a deep breath, and accept the invitation.

Here's the bottom line about fear: We have been conditioned to believe *God* is the one who plays it safe. We have cautioned our children and our spouses and our neighbors and our small group friends to sit tight and to leave the adventure to someone else. We have convinced ourselves it's best to get out of this life and into heaven by taking as few risks as possible. We have tightened our seat belts and worn our helmets and washed our hands until they are raw. We have filtered our air and our water and our perspective, and we have let the fear of what might go wrong lead us down the path of insignificance.

We feel a stirring in our heart to stop short of driving straight into the garage at the end of the day. So we toy with the idea of stopping in the driveway instead of driving into the garage and closing the door behind us. We tentatively consider making a slight adjustment to our daily routine by parking in the driveway so we can interact with our neighbor. But fear of what to say keeps us pressing the garage door opener without anything more than a passing wave at the person in the yard next door.

We are drawn to pray for communities on the "other side of the tracks," and we wonder if God really means for things to stay that way. But then we wonder if it's safe for us to go there and if we'd be welcomed, and so we write a check from the comfort of our great room with the open concept kitchen, and we never consider checking the little box on the form saying we'd like to know if there are other ways to help.

We desire to invite that new family at church to come home with us for dinner. But we don't trust our cooking or the cleanliness of our home or our ability to find something in common with people who don't look like us. So we smile and shake hands and say, "We should get together one day," and life goes on and on and on the way it always has, with the same number of places set at the table today as there were yesterday.

Ask a few people what they think is the opposite of fear, and they may say something like courage or bravery or peace or confidence or freedom. It is true. We want to live lives of courage. We want to be brave. We want to be peacemakers. We want to be confident that our lives matter and that our being here will make a difference in the long run. We want to be free of our fear and our guilt and the lies that trip us up and render us silent and apathetic and ineffective. We want to step off the drop-off and not be in over our heads. We wonder how to get to the opposite of fear.

We need a vaccine against the fears of this world. We need an antidote for our trembling hearts. Fear has fooled us into thinking it's too big to conquer, but the prescription is closer than we often realize.

The best way to get through fear (and I say "through" on purpose, because I suspect many of us will never really get *over* or even *out* of it; fear will always rise up to meet us as we make our way on the journey) is to press yourself right up to the very edge of the drop-off and then go one very small step further—right out into what looks like absolute nothingness from your current vantage point.

One of the biggest reasons I was able to get myself out into that ocean with the atrocious yellow life preserver encircling my hips had nothing at all to do with that life preserver. The main reason I was able to get myself out into that ocean was because of my trust in Harry and his love and concern for me. Over twenty-eight years of marriage, he has proven to me—time and time again—that I can trust him. But even Harry's love for me over all these years pales in comparison to the love God has for me and the degree to which I can absolutely trust God's love and concern for me.

I believed Harry when he said the yellow life preserver would hold me up. I took him at his word when he said I wouldn't drown. I trusted him.

Trust is the pathway through fear.

God invites us to reach out and put our hand into the hand he's holding out to us. That one little act—reaching out to God and trusting him to safely lead—can mean the difference between standing on the shore and soaring through what seems like outer space.

If trust is the pathway through fear, what is the pathway to trust? Trust is not a passive activity. It is not a spectator sport. Standing on the shore, saying with my words that I trusted Harry, would never yield the same result as actually putting my hand in his and taking that one small step into the deep. Saying I trust my husband is not the same as putting my hand in his and giving in to where the next step might lead.

Is it not the same with God? When we say we put our trust in him—that we have chosen to have faith in him—it's not the same as actually putting our hand in his and letting him take the lead in all things, is it? We build up our trust in God over days and weeks and months and years by following him through one small event after another after another. We have done this trust-building thing with family members and with friendships and with our spouses and our bosses and employees. Over time, in all of these relationships, the trust-worthiness of each of the significant people in our lives has been tested, through different situations and circumstances.

It happens quite naturally. We get sick and we learn that we can trust our spouse to care for us in the darkest hours of the night, without complaint and with hands that offer tender consolation. We are assigned a new project at work, and we learn that we can trust our employer to provide the needed resources and to mentor us through the parts of the project that lead us into uncovered territory. We purchase a new house, and we learn that we can trust our friends to show up with their strong backs and their pickup trucks and their extraordinary packing and organizing skills.

Our friendships and our marriages and the confidence with which we navigate our roles in the workplace are built, over time and through various experiences together, on the trust we find in one another. One small exchange after another helps us know where we can find our footing. We craft a history together, and it tells a tale of faithfulness and love and trustworthiness.

However, in these relationships with other human beings, the reverse is also true. Not every relationship is strong on trust. We learn where we can lean the heaviest, and we learn where to back off or step up to fill in the gap. We figure out exactly where we need to take the lead, and we discover when we need to look for help in other places. Sometimes we even realize it's time to walk away.

It's easy to look at God and navigate your relationship with him in the same way you navigate those relationships where trust is hard to find: bracing against disappointment, keeping track of who did what to whom, or feeling like the only person you can really trust in this relationship is you.

Sometimes it's easy to look around and make the declaration that God cannot be trusted after all. If we measure God's faithfulness to us by our bank account or our prognosis or the line we've been told to sign on the divorce decree, we might make the quick and easy choice to remain on the shore, undisturbed by shifting currents, at least until the tide comes in. Looking at events around us, we may often be tempted to fold our arms across our chests and announce to the dog at our feet, in no uncertain terms, "God didn't come through for me." But looking at what we can see and using that to make a judgment about the faithfulness of God would be shortsighted and ill-advised. What would happen if we were to dig a little deeper?

One year, in the midst of a particularly dark season of life, I felt compelled to somehow commemorate each occasion where it was clear to me that God was at work in my life or in the world around me. Through a series of events I no longer remember, a small garden planter filled with stones appeared on our front porch. When I decided to mark the moments where God had come through for me, I thought I would take one of the stones from that planter and place it on a tree stump just outside our back door. I didn't have high hopes for this particular project. I thought the moments of God's goodness in my life were nonexistent, so I had no aspirations of any noteworthy results taking place from this particular project. In retrospect, I can tell you I was underestimating things. Indeed, I was underestimating God.

Before the sun went down that day, I'd made two or three trips from the front porch to retrieve a stone and then through the house and out the back door to deposit that stone on the tree stump, marking a specific moment in time where it had been made clear to me that God was at work in the world, and that God *is* at work in the world, and that God *will be* at work in the world, and that I can trust him. Over days and weeks and months and seasons, I continued to mark the moments of God's faithfulness, and before I knew it, I had a growing pile of stones on the tree trunk. Visitors to our home began to ask about the pile of stones because they were clearly there for a reason. And when I washed the dishes or walked out the back door to water the tomato plants, there it was: proof to me that God can be trusted. God is at work, even when all seems lost and hope is hanging on by a thread.

"The sin underneath all our sins is to trust the lie of the serpent that we cannot trust the love and grace of Christ and must take matters into our own hands." Many people attribute these words to Martin Luther, though we can't be sure. Regardless of their origin, however, the words ring true, even today. From the beginning, however it was we came to believe the lie that God cannot be trusted ("Did God really say . . .?"; Gen. 3:1 NIV), we've been working our way back to trusting in God.

We build trust in God by putting matters back into his hands, one small moment at a time. We build trust in God by taking one small step in his direction and finding out he will always be there to catch us. It's easy to look out over the vastness of the Pacific Ocean and panic at the sight of such great power. The same is true with all the grand and glorious things that stretch out before you and threaten to consume you in your one amazing life, and so you keep standing on the shore. The headlines and conventional wisdom would shout to us that we must figure out a way to gather up the entire ocean of all that stretches out before us and tuck it neatly into our back pocket, and that notion is enough to terrify or overwhelm or threaten anyone.

One step is all that's needed, and you can trust God to take it with you. Before you know it, you'll have your own pile of smooth stones, piled up in remembrance and inviting you to trust that God goes with you into all things, and the waters will not pass over you.

Part 2

Following God's Leading

★ ⁂ ★ ★ ★ ★ **4** ★ ★ ★ ★ ⁂ ★

You Want Me to Go Where?

> Simply put, if you're not willing to take what is dearest to you, whether plans or people, and kiss it good-bye, you can't be my disciple. Salt is excellent. But if the salt goes flat, it's useless, good for nothing. Are you listening to this? Really listening?
>
> Jesus (Luke 14:33–35)

I've heard people say, "Whatever you take into the forest, you will find in the forest." By that they mean if you go into a new situation expecting it to be negative, that's how it will shake out. But if you go into a new situation and expect a positive experience, that's what you'll get.

We moved from Pennsylvania to Nebraska in 2005, while Hurricane Katrina was devastating New Orleans. We loaded our little Ford Escape to the brim—and then some, finally caving to the pressure of all our stuff and buying a soft-sided cartop carrier to help manage some of the overflow. It was August, and I stood on the running board of that blue SUV, pulling tightly on the canvas straps of the cartop carrier, doing my best to make sure we didn't lose any of our belongings somewhere on the road between the perfectly acceptable Philadelphia suburb we were leaving and the flat, foreboding, unforgiving prairie wasteland on the Great Plains of the American Midwest.

I was not feeling good about this move. There had been lots of tears and arguments and misunderstandings in the weeks leading up to the decision to relocate. But Harry was excited about returning to local church ministry after four years working as a consultant for our denomination. I couldn't blame him. He was (and is) uniquely gifted for this particular ministry in this particular church and with this particular congregation. When he talked about local church ministry, there was no way to deny the excitement in his eyes or the eagerness he had for beginning this new season.

But Nebraska?

I suspect you may have your own Nebraska. Perhaps you have a place you don't ever want to go, a person you'd rather not have your child marry, a job you'd prefer were assigned to someone other than you, or an experience you'd rather not endure. Some of you can point to your Nebraska without hesitation. You're not necessarily proud of it, but you know the limits of your grace and mercy, and you are comfortable with your relationship with God, as long as he understands

78

that certain places and people and tasks and experiences are off-limits for you. If you're like me, you trust God not to cross the boundaries you've established, and up until now, he's been respectful of those lines you've drawn around yourself.

When I travel and meet new people, it's only a matter of time before someone asks, "So where do you live, Deidra?" I tell them, and their faces get this strange expression—a cross between a blank stare and utter surprise. I have lived a lot of places, but Nebraska is the only one that elicits this response.

"Have you been to Nebraska?" I ask, keeping up the polite conversation. Ninety-nine percent of the time, they answer like this: "I've been *through* Nebraska" (usually on their way to Colorado) or "I've flown *over* Nebraska" (usually on their way to Anyplace Else). Nebraska is not on the top of very many people's destination lists.

I totally get it. Believe me. When Harry first told me about Nebraska, we were in a rented Chevy Malibu hatchback, driving from Pennsylvania to a friend's wedding in Birmingham, Alabama. I think Harry knew it would be best to give me this news in a place where I couldn't get away and where I'd be able to scream, if necessary, without being heard.

"There's a church in Nebraska," Harry told me, his eyes on the road toward Birmingham.

"Oh yeah?" I answered, thinking he was making polite conversation.

"Yeah," he replied. "They're looking for a pastor."

"That's nice," I said, thinking he wanted me to add them to my prayer list. Where was that prayer list, anyway? Finding a pastor is no easy task. "Have they been looking long?" I asked.

"Yes. I first heard about them a year ago," he said, his hands on the steering wheel at driver's ed ten and two.

Wait a minute, I was thinking in my best Jerry Seinfeld voice. My brain was catching on.

"I'm thinking I might put my name in for consideration," Harry was saying.

I may have laughed out loud. I know I was laughing in my head; laughing to keep from throwing open the door of that Chevy Malibu and running across the highway and then heading east—as far away from Nebraska as I could possibly get.

But what I said was, "Are there people there?"

Now he was the one laughing. "Yes," he said. "There are people there."

"Are there black people there?" I pressed, narrowing the playing field.

When it came to Nebraska, I was clueless. I am not exaggerating when I tell you I had to look up Nebraska on the map. I asked all the questions people ask who have never been to this part of this country: Are there any cities? Is everyone a farmer? Are there more cows or more people? Is there electricity? Indoor plumbing?

I know, I know.

Eventually, I found an official-looking website, which helped to clue me in. It contained some of the data compiled from the most recent census. I scanned the site for information about cost of living, employment opportunities, and quality of education and air, and then, in the demographics section, I learned Nebraska's population is 3 percent black. I remember staring at that number, trying to figure out what it meant in terms of living a real life in Nebraska, as a real person in brown skin. Would there be anyone there who looked like me? Would anyone be able to help me find someone to do my hair? Would I always be the only person in the crowd with brown skin? The numbers from the census didn't give me confidence. Even allowing for changes in the years since the census had been taken, it was unlikely that number had gained an additional 30 or 40 percentage points. Or even 7 percentage points.

So there was that. And that might be part of the explanation behind that odd facial response I get from people when I tell them where I live. They look at my brown skin and naturally coiled hair, and perhaps they ask themselves some of the very same questions I asked. Or maybe they're just thinking, "Where is Nebraska, anyway?"

As you may have surmised, Harry did put his name in for that church in Nebraska, and they quickly called to invite us out for an interview. I remember feeling, through the entire weekend we were in Nebraska for that interview, as if I had been transported to an alternate reality. The sky was enormous; the heat sweltered up from everywhere and threatened to melt me right there on the sidewalk. I was completely out of my element. But I somehow naively avoided entertaining any thoughts about what it would be like to actually live in Nebraska and to join my life with the people of this congregation in this specific city. I placated myself with the knowledge that come Sunday afternoon, I'd be on an airplane back to Pennsylvania and the real life that happened to be working quite well for me, thank you very much.

But that first interview turned into a second interview, and before I knew it, we had sold our house in Pennsylvania, bought a house in Nebraska, enrolled our children in school (Did I mention our son was entering his senior year of high school? If you gasped, you're not alone. People always gasp when I tell them that part.), and now here I was, standing on the running board of my vehicle, tightening the strap on a canvas cartop carrier and waving good-bye over the hood of the car to the people who had been my neighbors for the previous four years.

If I had heard the news about the impending hurricane, I would have known for sure what I already felt in my heart: this move was not going to go well.

You may not actually be aware of the existence of your own Nebraska until it shows up at your front door. You may be sensing God extending a hand to you, and when you look out in the direction of where he seems to be headed, it doesn't look like anything you'd ever wish for. In fact, it might look completely terrifying and uncomfortable and barren and dry. You might try to find a way to decline this particular invitation from God without hurting his feelings or causing an unfortunate domino effect.

It doesn't matter who you are, how many places you've lived, how old you are, how much you believe God is good all the time and all the time God is good. Moving your entire life from one culture to another culture is a challenge. And when I say *challenge*, I want you to envision that word not only italicized but also in all caps, bolded, underlined, and in seventy-gazillion font size. With an exclamation mark.

The same is true about moving forward into what God is calling you to do. Sometimes it's beautiful and easy, and it's what you've been waiting for, for as long as you can remember. But it's not always that way. Sometimes, moving forward with God is the biggest challenge you will ever face. You will want to fight it with all you've got in you, and you will analyze it from every possible angle. You may look for the emergency exit, fully aware that the nearest exit might be behind you. You might put your fingers in your ears and sing loudly, drowning out the still, small voice of God. You will want to find a way around it. You will ask people to pray you out of it instead of through it. "How can this possibly be God's idea?" you might whisper into a cold, dark night. "I didn't sign up for this. I am not the person for this job." Sometimes moving forward with God takes its toll on a person. We are wise to count the cost.

I was used to moving. Moving a family and a household from one place to another has its own set of challenges, from getting your children settled in a new school to staying on the phone for hours, trying to get someone to come out to your house and set up the cable line for you. But within a few months, you find a church or a book club or a neighborhood playgroup or a group of co-workers who get you and who make you feel at home, and your world starts spinning on its axis again. Your children adjust, you get Wi-Fi, you figure out how to DVR your favorite television shows, and your new friends invite you to girls' night out. You invite people to your house for dinner. You decide the grocery store around the corner is your new favorite and the way people drive in this new place is irritating but tolerable. You exhale. You smile. Your family begins to thrive.

That's not how it happened for us in Nebraska. There were small things, like the heat and the wild and unpredictable storms, which threw trees down on our house, tore off the pillars of our front porch, and left a gaping hole in our roof. There were the mice that took up residence in our pantry. And there was the wind. On the first Sunday in our new church, I stood in front of the building on the sidewalk, trying to keep my skirt from going all Marilyn Monroe on me (*that* would

have been a memorable introduction from the pastor's wife)
while holding up a hand to keep my hair from slicing through
my eyeballs. A woman came and stood next to me, expres-
sionless, her gaze fixed on nothing in particular. "The wind
here," she said, all on one note. "There's no use fighting it."

But there were also bigger things. People started leaving the
church in droves, without so much as a parting handshake.
One Sunday they'd be there, and the next Sunday they were
gone, reminding me somehow of the vintage computer game
version of The Oregon Trail. We had no way to know what
was making them leave. Was it doctrine? Theology? And as
always, we had to wonder if it had something to do with the
color of our skin. But who asks questions like those?

Whatever you take into the forest . . .

I'd have conversations with people, thinking I'd commu-
nicated clearly, only to be disappointed the following week
when I learned I had not been understood at all, nor had I
understood. Harry says it was like picking up an object in his
hands and finding it was really just sand, slipping through
his fingers.

We questioned whether or not we'd heard God correctly,
and I kept going back in my mind to all the bad feelings
I'd had about this move—right from the beginning. I cried.
We grew silent. We were constantly on edge, waiting for the
other shoe to drop. Harry became more and more defeated
with each passing day. I started having panic attacks every
Sunday morning.

And that was just the church.

Nebraska took our entire world, turned it upside down,
and shook it out like a feather pillow in the jaws of an angry
dog. Nebraska shook us out like that, and then the Nebraska

84

winds picked up the feathers of our lives and scattered them to what seemed like the four corners of the earth.

I could barely talk without crying. I fell into bed each night exhausted, defeated, and depressed.

"Whatever you take into the forest, you will find in the forest." I'm sure there may have been some of that at work in our situation. I expected the move to go poorly, and I am sure some of that attitude spilled over into the actual experience of this particular life transition. I'll take responsibility for that. But I don't think I can blame my attitude for the winters in Nebraska.

That first winter, the snow fell and fell and fell. And then it fell some more. The street at the end of our driveway was impassable, and it was all Harry could do to keep the driveway clear. He spent days on end pushing the snow blower up and down the driveway, piling up snowdrifts so high they reached the gutters, and icicles from the roof poked steely fingers down through the sloped ridges of those drifts. Our son dug a tunnel into the drifts, building an actual room that a full-grown adult could walk into and stand upright inside.

Snow melted from the roof and seeped down through the wall between the kitchen and the family room, peeling back the outer shell of the drywall and taunting Harry to sand and tape and putty and paint—over and over again. The ceiling at the bottom of the staircase from our bedroom pooled with water from the roof—greeting me with little droplets of water hanging at eye level when I descended the stairs in the morning. We kept a bucket at the bottom of the stairs to catch the drips.

The windows of our house were drafty enough that the curtains moved when the icy winds blew outside, even though the sash on each window was locked tight. But the sliding door to the patio wouldn't close all the way, and snow drifted into the living room, piling up on the white shag carpet the former owners had left behind.

We still wonder how that house ever passed inspection.

We stood in front of the bay window, wrapped in layers of clothes in an attempt to keep warm, and watched the snow pile up outside. After a few days, we wondered if anyone was ever going to come and rescue us. We hadn't seen anything but massive pickup trucks or SUVs with enormously thick and nubby tires gain any sort of traction on the road outside our home. "When are the plows coming?" I asked Harry.

When they finally came, the snowplows scraped what appeared to be an inch or two of snow off the incredibly impressive layers that had accumulated in the never-ending snowfall. And then, it seemed, those snowplows deposited that snow right at the end of our driveway: our own personal welcome mat. I took it personally, anyway. I may have had a meltdown. What can I say?

I started planning my escape. I wanted out. Not through.

As far as I could tell, Nebraska was the very worst place to live in all the world. Here's how I saw it: The people were peculiar. The landscape was ugly. The shopping was a challenge, and not in a good way—I had to drive an hour just to buy cosmetics that matched my skin tone. The teachers in my children's school were strange. And I haven't even mentioned the obsession with football. Oh my goodness! The football!

That first football season we lived in Nebraska, I went to run some errands on a Saturday afternoon, and on that day, the city of Lincoln was like a ghost town. Very few cars were on the roads, and hardly anyone was in line at the grocery store. I didn't have to worry about finding a parking place. I felt like I was in an early episode of *The Walking Dead* or something. Or that odd end-times/rapture movie they used to show at church youth camp to scare teenagers into saying the sinner's prayer. On that Saturday, all of the people I did see were wearing red. Every single one of them. I started to wonder if I'd missed a memo. These people do not mess around when it comes to Cornhuskers football. It's as if football is a religion and the Cornhuskers are a denomination. Nebraskans are die-hard fans. I've never seen anything like it. For me, it was unsettling. It was yet another layer to a culture with which I was completely unfamiliar and which left me feeling isolated and adrift.

I had to get out of there before that guy from *The Twilight Zone* walked into my kitchen with a cigarette in his hand.

I've heard people say seven is God's number of completion. I don't know where that comes from. I don't even know if it's true. But it would take seven years—seven windy summers, seven ice-riddled winters, seven football seasons, seven years of Sundays—before Nebraska started to feel like home. For most of those seven years, I tried to get out of Nebraska. I prayed. I searched for jobs in other states. I encouraged my husband to apply to different churches, or to become a mail carrier—calling be damned! I searched the internet to determine the cost of living in places like Ohio and Colorado and New York City. I considered what it would be like to move in with my parents. I begged God for a reprieve, and when no doors opened, I gave God the silent treatment, silently shaking my fist at him and vowing to get revenge for his decision to zip his lips, throw away the key, and ignore me.

I beat my fist against the dark and turned my back on the wilderness. I wanted no part of this foolishness.

Years before, in a church sanctuary filled with women in astoundingly beautiful hats and men in three-piece suits and Stacy Adams shoes, I'd stood in the pew and sang along with the choir and the Hammond organ and the drums. We waved our arms above our heads or clapped our hands on two and four, and we threw back our heads, exposing our very throats and hearts to God, and we belted out songs about Jesus, the Light of the World.

For all those years in Nebraska, I couldn't find the light. It was as if I'd find a box of matches in my kitchen pantry, the corner of the box gnawed through by mice, and fumble with frozen fingers to strike a single wooden match against the flint. Just as the spark danced in front of my eyes, that unforgiving wind swooped in and snuffed it out, leaving me with the heavy scent of sulfur in my nostrils.

Have you been in dark places like that too? Have you found yourself huddled against the cold, your back turned to God and your hands balled into fists and stuffed into the pockets of your overcoat? Has your voice gone raspy from lamenting and crying out to God for a way out? Have you wondered where you went wrong and what you did to deserve this? Have you slunk back into the shadows, convinced you've gotten exactly what you deserved and that the light of day was never meant for you? Maybe you have silently whispered curses to the God of your salvation? You are not alone.

One of my favorite stories in the Bible is found in the sixteenth chapter of Exodus. It's one of my favorites now because I'm on the other side of that story. You know how, when you're experiencing a difficult time, sometimes someone will say something like "You'll get through this"? And it is true. You will. It's the getting through that beats the crap out of you, though, isn't it? So when I was in the middle of my first seven years in Nebraska and I was getting the crap beat out of me, I would not have been pleased to have someone share this little Exodus chapter 16 story with me. If a preacher had started a sermon with these verses, I'd have politely gathered up my belongings and exited that sanctuary, convinced God was playing some sort of cruel joke on me.

In the book of Exodus, Moses had been exiled from Egypt and had settled into life on the back side of the desert. The people of God, who were enslaved and enduring incomprehensible conditions under the rule of Pharaoh, were looking for a way out too. They cried out to God and asked God to deliver them out of their predicament. They were through with being slaves and with being ridiculed and mistreated. They were done with living as if they were less-than when they knew in their heart of hearts that they were God's chosen people. They looked at their situation and believed something better for themselves. They wanted out, and God heard their cries.

By the time we reach the sixteenth chapter of Exodus, the people of God have been released from bondage in Egypt. Along with a mixed multitude of people, they left Egypt and their enslavement behind them, and they crossed through the Red Sea on dry ground. Dry ground! Just as they had requested, they had been delivered. God had led them out—an incredible pillar of cloud pointing the way in the daytime and an equally incredible pillar of fire pointing the way at night. These were God's people. God had heard their cry and answered their prayer for freedom. And now, halfway through the second month of their deliverance and smack dab in the middle of what was called the Wilderness of Sin, this group of people realized they were hungry.

They began whining and complaining, and they turned their backs toward the wilderness, and they begged for deliverance from their deliverance. "Take us back to Egypt," they demanded. "We're hungry out here! At least in Egypt we had food to eat!" Whine, whine, whine. Complain, complain, complain. Curse, curse, curse. They pouted. They cursed some more. They stomped their feet. They probably shook their fists.

At some point—because of God's great love for these people who would get on anyone else's last nerve—God told Moses to tell Aaron to tell the people that food was on its way. Food would rain down from the skies, and the people would no longer be hungry. So Aaron gathered the people to deliver the news, and here's what it says in Exodus 16, verse 10:

> When Aaron gave out the instructions to the whole company of Israel, *they turned to face the wilderness*. And there it was: the Glory of GOD visible in the Cloud. (emphasis added)

What is your wilderness? What is it that you've been resisting? Where is that place you've told God you will not go? Who is that person you've vowed to never forgive, never welcome in, never extend grace toward? Would you be willing to reconsider?

All those years in Nebraska, I kept my back to the wilderness, searching for the light in all the wrong places, when God was right there in the wilderness—visible in the cloud. His invitation to me was an invitation into the wilderness, and I used every ounce of energy at my disposal to resist his advances. Have you done that too? Many times God's invitations are not at all what we'd expect them to be. They don't look the way we thought they would. They often look risky and windy and icy and cold, and they take us to the very furthest reaches of everything we think we know or want to know. And then they stretch us further than that. Beyond our self-imposed limits. We see the darkness and we forget even darkness is light to God.

We might even convince ourselves God couldn't possibly be there in the wilderness. But we couldn't be further from the truth.

When I wasn't looking, when I was complaining and whining and stomping my feet and shaking my fists and giving God the silent treatment, God had already placed his hands on my shoulders and was slowly and ever so imperceptibly turning me to face the wilderness. Inch by inch. One small, loving, patient gesture after another. God used people at our church to get through to me. He sent me opportunities for work that I never would have encountered anywhere but in Nebraska. God sent nourishment to me, right in the middle of the wilderness. Eventually—and for this, I will always thank God—I gave in.

When you drive into Nebraska, on your way to Colorado or Anyplace Else, you'll see a sign welcoming you to Nebraska. "The Good Life," it reads. When we first moved here, I'd think about that sign and say, "Surely that slogan was outsourced. It's not possible someone who actually lives in Nebraska would say that about Nebraska!"

Then, one summer afternoon just a few weeks before the seventh anniversary of our move to Nebraska, I was riding my bike on a street in a neighborhood downtown. No one else was on the street, but I clearly heard someone say, "This is the good life."

I looked around to see who'd said that. I saw no one, because *I* was the one who said it.

Yes. *Me.*

How could this be? How had I changed my mind about Nebraska? *When* had I changed my mind about Nebraska? What in the world had come over me? I don't know how you feel about miracles these days. I don't know if you've made up your mind that God doesn't work that way anymore—that he's done being all fancy with us the way he used to be in the Bible. I don't know if you've been duped into thinking miracles are only for the rich and famous or for preachers on television. Say what you will about miracles, but before you do, let me tell you it could only have been a miracle that changed the state of my heart in the state of Nebraska.

I kept my secret to myself for quite a while. I didn't dare tell anyone I had grown soft for Nebraska. But on the inside, I found myself marveling at the astounding vastness of the cornflower blue skies that unfurled each morning right over my head. I was captivated by the way the sunlight skipped around on actual amber waves of grain. I hiked trails through the prairie and took my time, gazing at columbine and prairie grass and monarch butterflies feeding on goldenrod. I rode my bicycle on miles and miles of straight, flat trails, with cluttered thoughts falling from my mind with each round of the pedals and frogs singing to me from the tall grasses that lined the trail. I stood stock-still and watched the most fantastic sunset and then turned in the other direction and practically fell into the harvest moon. I camped in a tent on a cot next to Harry in one of those wild and thunderous storms, praying God would let us make it through the night without being consumed by lightning, and when we unzipped the tent the next morning, pearl crescent butterflies swarmed us and rested on my shoulders and on my bicycle helmet and on my thigh, as if God were telling me he'd been there all along. He had never missed a beat.

Nothing had changed about Nebraska. The storms and the sunsets and the harvest moons and the pearl crescent butterflies had always been there. But spending time in the middle of the wilderness had changed me. Isn't that the way it goes? God loves us too much to leave us where he finds us. He has a vision in his mind of who we were meant to be, and he has his mind set on getting us there, one small step at a time. Some of those steps may take us to places we'd rather not go. But remember, the glory of God is *in* the wilderness. As much as we want to resist it, in the wilderness of our lives, God works to transform us more and more into the image of his Son and a reflection of his character.

One day, while I was driving a stretch of highway with the sun setting to my right, I had this silly little thought that someone ought to have a conference in Nebraska for all those people who can't get to the conferences on the coasts but who have an amazing dream and who might like to get together with others who dream amazing dreams. Because, I thought, Nebraska is just the place a person can hear from God and get inspired.

It was a good idea, so I started sharing it with people I knew who know how to make things happen. They are the detail people, the networkers and thinkers, the ones with a Plan A *and* a Plan B. They take great delight in spreadsheets and logistics and strategies and details. I shared my idea with the

93

detail people, and they looked at me with genuine and sincere interest and affirmation in their eyes. They agreed with me, weighing the pros and cons and saying it was true—someone really ought to have a conference in Nebraska because it's just the place a person can hear from God and get inspired. But they didn't bite and say, "I think I'm supposed to make that happen!" So the idea sat idle in my mind.

But then I shared my silly little idea with people I know who see the beauty of an idea before you've even finished your sentence. They are the dreamers. They aren't stymied by lack of resources or time or energy. "The sky's the limit!" they shout in gleeful unison. They move through the world like music, and it seems as if they sing songs with their bodies—full of grace and hopefulness. They raise a glass of champagne to toast the end of an ordinary day. They are paint-ers and sculptors and writers and dancers, and they agreed with me—wiping paint on their blue jeans and turning up the music just a notch. Someone ought to have a conference in Nebraska because it's just the place a person can hear from God and get inspired. But they didn't bite and say, "I think I'm supposed to make that happen!" So the idea sat idle in my mind.

When I say the idea sat idle in my mind, what I really mean is that it danced around in there, not giving up, not wind-ing down, not going away. It wasn't annoying. Don't get me wrong. It was just . . . present. It was like the sound of wind chimes on the back porch of a house around the corner. Steady and melodious. It didn't demand attention, but it didn't stop playing its tune.

One day I was driving south, the sun setting in the west, the sky on fire like that burning bush in Exodus, and I said to

God, "So what about that conference idea? You know? That little idea you gave me that no one wants to do? When are you going to find someone to make that happen?"

God is so polite. So gentle. So patient and kind. God is love. Looking back on that moment from this vantage point, I imagine God letting out a little sound between a scoff and a sigh.

Now, if I tell you here that God spoke to me, you'll have your own idea of what that means. I can't say I've ever heard God's voice, but I do think we tend to diminish the possibility that God might actually speak to us in these days of MP4s and text messaging and the wireless handheld devices we call phones. We've pretty much got the whole communication thing on lockdown. Heck, I have a degree in communication! But this communication with God is something altogether different.

Yes, God spoke to me. But not with words. And not necessarily in a way I can describe. It was more than polite conversation, where we simply skim the surface while hoping the music will start already so we can both focus on something else.

I have found someone, God "said" to me.

In my response to him, I may have stuttered. "If there is one thing I know, it's that I am not the person for that job," I answered. "I'm not into details and spreadsheets. I don't have connections. I've never planned an event of this size. I am simply me. I'm not a rock star or an arena speaker. I don't have the skills for this."

As it turns out, that is just the type of résumé that makes us God's perfect candidate. When we've allowed the wilderness experience to strip us down to "simply me," we are just the right size for God's big plans.

You know how sometimes God asks you to do the very thing that scares you most? You know how we sometimes say stuff like, "I want to let God be in control, really, I do. But what if God makes me move to Nebraska or something?"

Then, realizing what we've done, we look up to the sky, or wherever it is we think God is listening from, and we say, "Just kidding, God," because we know the minute we tell God what we don't want to do, it's as if God takes special note of that and somehow works it into our lifetime schedule of events.

We talk about God-sized dreams, and a lot of us imagine that to mean some big, grand gesture God is asking us to make. Sometimes I get lost in the dreamy prospects of the thing. But if I'm honest, I have to tell you that a God-sized dream might surprise you because of its smallness. It will push you to the very edge of your comfort zone and right into the desolation of the wilderness. And it won't always stop there.

Here's the thing about the terrifying parts of following God's invitation into the wilderness: even though you're so afraid you think you might pass out and throw up at the same time, right where you stand, God is good and God is in control. The wilderness is uniquely suited for putting us in a situation where God can get a hearing from us. Without resources, stretched far beyond our abilities, and with hope consigned to the garbage bin, we want out of the wilderness, but God desires to bring us *through*. And he is right there with us. He doesn't send us into the wilderness and wait for us to emerge on the other side. No. God walks every step of the wilderness journey with us, and he shapes us as we make our way our through. We are softer in the wilderness, despite our best intentions.

In the end, we had that conference. I was the one God chose to invite on that particular adventure. And it was beautiful. Of course, there were about sixty different occasions where I was convinced the whole thing would kill me (I know, I'm so dramatic). But it was beautiful. "Life changing," "My watershed moment," "Exactly what I needed," the attendees said when it was all said and done. Who knew?

God is in the wilderness. Go there. You can trust him to meet you right in the middle of your wild and worn and weary places. Take off your shoes. Tear off your pretense. Skip over the polite conversation. It's you he wants. Simply you.

Shake your fist and stomp your feet and whine, whine, whine, because it's you he wants. Just the way you are. He's got designs on you. He will catch your eye across a crowded room and tell your entire story without ever speaking a word, and when you're driving south with the sky on fire like a burning bush, your heart will hear his gentle whisper in the deepest places.

Maybe what he says will sound a bit like this:

Welcome to the good life.

✯ ✰ ✯ ✯ ✯ ✯ **5** ✯ ✯ ✯ ✯ ✯ ✯

Breathlessness

I'll breathe my life into you and you'll live.

God (Ezek. 37:14)

Early on frigid mornings in Nebraska, when the sun is trying to decide whether it will share a few rays to keep us warm, I am sometimes the one who slides open the back door and stands on the deck to let the dog run past me into the yard. If there is no frost on the ground, I may step out in my socks and exhale into the air to see my breath. Those are the only days I can point to an actual visual representation of the air circulating in my lungs to keep me upright and alive. We can't see the air we're breathing, but we know it is there. And we know when it is absent.

We have seen the sobering evidence of breathlessness.

One night when our daughter was sixteen months old, I awoke to the sound of my husband rushing past me and through the family room, then swinging open the door to the room where our daughter slept. "What's going on?" I called out into the darkness.

"She's not breathing," my husband answered as he rushed right out the door and outside, holding our daughter to his chest. It was happening too quickly for me to be terrified. I jumped up and turned on the light. "I'm taking her to the emergency room," my husband said. And then he was gone. Just like that, the red lights of our vehicle getting smaller in the darkness.

On that night, there were no cell phones to keep us tethered to one another. No email. No social media. No text messages. Nothing. I checked on our son, who takes after his mother and can sleep through almost anything. Then I sat in the middle of the bed, a pink blanket covering me and the beige rotary dial telephone in my lap, right in the middle of the sea of pink blanket folds. I rested my hand on the receiver and willed it to ring.

Silence.

In moments like these, some would say, the right and good and spiritual thing is probably to pray. I imagine perhaps those people would be right. But what does one say when one would simply like to breathe?

Our daughter spent ten days in the hospital under an oxygen tent. Her recovery was slow but steady. My husband and I took turns alternating between sleeping on the hospital floor and taking care of our son, who ate sherbet when he visited his tiny sister in her cavernous hospital room. Later, when things settled down, my husband told me that on the night our daughter stopped breathing, he strapped Alexandra into the front seat of the car and ran every red light between our house and the hospital in town, bargaining with God with each click of the odometer. "God," he whispered into the air, "if you take her tonight, I will trust you. I will be angry. I will be lost. But I will trust you."

When each of our children was born, we dressed our new baby in a white gown and went to church. Our pastor held them in his arms, and there in front of God, the congregation, and each other, on each occasion, my husband and I dedicated those babies back to God. We promised to do our best to raise them to know God, and the congregation stood to their feet and vowed to walk beside us on the journey. Three times the pastor gently touched the tips of his fingers to the forehead of the infant in his arms as he dedicated that child back to God in the name of the Father (touch), and of the Son (touch), and of the Holy Spirit (touch). Our intent, standing there at the front of the church in our Sunday best, was to give these children back to God, to do our best with what we had, and to acknowledge they were his first, entrusted to our care.

But it's one thing to stand in front of God and the entire church and make a promise. It's quite another thing to have God call you on that vow. So when my husband told me he had given Alexandra back to God in a speeding car on the way to the emergency room, I gasped a little on the inside. Who was he, I asked myself, to make such a big decision without first consulting me? Wasn't this our child? Together? Didn't I get a say in the matter? Didn't I get a veto?

My husband was right, though, of course. Our child's life is not ours to own, to direct, and to claim a right to, any more than I have a right to claim my own breath or life. Everything—the stars in the sky, the birds in their nests, the refrigerators in our kitchens—is entrusted to us from God. Every single bit of it, from the smallest thing to the biggest. This one race I'm running, this life I'm living, is a gift to me from God. And so is yours. Your life is a gift to you—and to the rest of us. You are a gift to us. The breath in your lungs is a gift to this world, and it is also an act of worship—a prayer of grace to God.

In Genesis 1, the word for the Spirit of God is translated to mean breath. It was the breath of God, hovering over and moving upon the face of the waters or, as other translations name it, the deep. In the story of creation, after all is said and done and God's dirt-caked hands hold a human form, it is this same breath that God imparts to us, and we become alive—living souls.

We are not God. We know this. We are well acquainted with our smallness, and in the moments we forget, it doesn't take long before we bump into the sobering reality of our humanity. But this is also true: we are intimately and exquisitely crafted by the God who gives us this one race to run. We should not underestimate the breath in our lungs and how it links us to the one who gives us life. Every breath we breathe is a gossamer testimony, rising toward the heavens. When everyone seems to be upping the ante and raising the qualifications for what it means to impact the world in meaningful ways or to live a significant life, we write our story with our breath and we make space on the earth for God.

Sometimes breathing is the only prayer we can pray, and God hears our sigh and once again breathes the breath of life into us. We exhale, and it seems like such a little thing. But some days it is everything. It is communion—intimate and more than breathing oxygen and exhaling carbon dioxide. It is sacred and it is holy: this agreeing with God that we need

God, for all of everything, and his joyful entering into our lives and ourselves and our very souls to make us one with him. We are gulping and breathing and sighing and gasping, and we realize our deep, deep hunger inside.

The biblical account of creation reveals an extremely intimate relationship between humanity and God. Out of silence and darkness, God speaks, creating light and water and wind and waves. God populates the earth with creatures that gallop and slither and hop across the ground. God fills the sea with eels and whales and starfish and catfish. God creates trees that bear fruit and grass that reaches into the soil and up toward the heavens. And then, from the ground, God crafts humanity.

Have you ever reached your hands down into the earth? Have you felt the warmth of the soil in the palm of your hands, the damp earth wrapping itself around your knees, your toes sinking into terra firma? Have you taken off your gardening gloves and welcomed the dirt to gather there beneath your nails and embed itself under your cuticles so that the next day, even though you scrubbed and showered and washed again, you look at your hands and see the soil still there beneath your nails?

Working the earth requires a bowed-down posture. Whether you stand up with your hands wrapped around a wooden handle, pulling the flat side of a hoe through the ground, or you get low and bend your knees—close enough to smell the dirt and to spy an earthworm just before it disappears beneath the surface—when crafting something from the earth, the head must be bowed to get a better look at the work of your hands. So it is that in the very beginning, we find God reaching out toward us.

The entirety of God's love toward us tells this story of God himself—all-knowing, all-powerful, all- and ever-present

God—bending toward us, reaching out in our direction, coming toward us before we even knew there was a difference between up and down. God loved us first, before we could rack up points or accomplishments or ever-increasing feats of genius to impress God and make him want to love us. We keep reaching, reaching, reaching up as if there is some ladder we should climb. Our vain attempts at getting God's attention and improving our rank belie the truth that God is love, and because he is, he couldn't help but love us first of all.

Throughout the telling of the story in the Pentateuch, the first five books of the Bible, we see God always and ever reaching toward us. He was there for Moses in a burning bush, lighting up the darkness and promising to be with Moses in the liberation of God's people. God was there with the lamb in the brambles, providing the perfect sacrifice for Abraham and for Isaac. God unfurled a stairway from heaven down to earth and held fast to Jacob, who walked away with a limp and a blessing from the Lord. God extended his hand to us through every story in every book of the Old Testament. And then, in the very first pages of the Gospels, God again reached down from the heavens and came to be with us, now as an infant in a stable with the livestock, behind a crowded inn. Shepherds and kings bowed down at the sight of him, but even then, it was God who'd made the first move.

"Like a mammy bending over her baby,"[1] God stoops down and bends over us, even now, just as he did the day he scooped a handful of clay from the earth and made of it a human form, letting the soil pack itself around his cuticles.

Genesis tells us the story of creation, numbering the events in categories we call days. All manner of living things were crafted from the spoken word of God—living trees and flowering plants and birds that fly and fish that swim and cows and dogs and ducks and llama, each one birthed into being by the Word of God and released into the world to make more of the same and to fill the earth.

But we're the only ones over whom God stooped low and pressed his knees into the earth and welcomed dirt beneath his fingernails and shaped us with his very hands. Ours are the bodies, created in his very image, beneath which God slid his hands while heavenly fragrances hung in the air and stars danced in the universe. We are the ones God himself lifted toward his heartbeat, and we are the only ones into whom God himself breathed the breath of life.

Did you just inhale?

Almighty God. He is the first and the last, the beginning and the end. This very same God bowed low to form us, and he also lifted us to himself to give us life.

We are the children of the living God. We didn't do a single thing to make that true. We didn't score extra points or run the fastest race. Before we were created, God chose breath for us. He chose it from the beginning, and he continues to choose breath for us; for you. He reaches out to us, and he lifts us to himself, giving us form and filling us with life.

There are days, or nights, or long stretches of weeks or months or even years, when breathing is the only prayer we've got. The breath of our lungs, given to us from the beginning and offered up as an act of worship. We inhale, and then we exhale. Each breath signs our names on the dotted line of de-pendence, whether we're thinking about it or not. We inhale so we can keep on going. And then we exhale, marking the cessation of striving and seeking, the end of struggling and sweating to be noticed and to win and to arrive. How long can you hold your breath? Eventually, you've got to let it go. We let go so we can live. It is a sweet surrender.

Inhale. Exhale. He is here. God, through the Holy Spirit, is present and active and alive today. All those years ago, when Jesus was making preparation for his death and resurrection, he introduced us anew to the Holy Spirit, saying the Holy Spirit would come to us and comfort us and remind us of all the things Jesus taught when he was among us. "I am alive," Jesus told the disciples that day, "and you're about to come alive" (John 14:19). The power of the Holy Spirit is life; it is like breath in our lungs. It is the Spirit of God, not just hovering over the waters and the deep, but now, at our behest and invitation, infused into our very being and dwelling *within* us. We cannot see him, but if we're paying attention, we know when he's there. Moving forward without first surrendering to the Holy Spirit leaves us spiritually breathless.

We feel this breathlessness when we charge ahead with our own plans and on our own strength. No matter the difficulty of the project or the uncertainty of its outcome, there is a noticeable difference where the Holy Spirit is absent. It may not be obvious to the rest of the team or to the audience or to the neighbors in the house next door. But when we move forward into the plans God has entrusted to us without first surrendering to the direction and power of the Holy Spirit, we risk the danger of delivering a product or a message that—no matter how successful in the eyes of conventional wisdom— fails to spark life, or to give life, or to point to life that will last beyond the quarterly sales figures or the dinner party we host for our next-door neighbors.

But how do we get there? How do we truly surrender our will and our way to his?

Many times we find ourselves forced into the surrender, running all the red lights in the middle of the night and breathing our letting go into the windshield as we press down on the gas pedal. Other times we make the decision and it's a ceremony, with our dreams and our goals and our desire for a life of significance dressed up in a fancy white gown and handed over for a blessing from the pastor and the Holy Trinity.

Here is a magnificent and true dichotomy: we cannot truly surrender to the Holy Spirit without the Holy Spirit first breathing surrender into us. It is a surrender unto surrender. We want to live a life of significance, but we can't live it until we release our hold on it. A life surrendered to the Spirit of God is a life lived with open hands, palms turned upward in letting go. We have to let go so we can live. It is tempting, though, to want to grab hold of the future God has for us and to think it belongs to us. Like Abraham and Sarah, we think we see where God is leading, and then we take the reins, calling in our concubines and creating our own version of the story.

Abraham and Sarah: pillars of the faith and heroes in the stories of the people of God. When we first meet them, their names are Abram and Sarai, and they are given a promise that their descendants will outnumber the grains of sand on the shore and the stars in the sky. Incredible! Fantastic! Abram was seventy-five years old when God spoke this promise to him. He and his bride, Sarai, were childless. And yet Abram believed God. But then God took his time, as God is prone to do, and I imagine Abram thought that God thought that maybe Abram ought to do his part to make the promise a reality. So when Sarai suggested Abram sleep with her maid, Hagar, Abram agreed and did what Sarai suggested. From the union of Abram and Hagar, Hagar became pregnant, and we are told that Hagar rubbed it in whenever she got a chance, taunting Sarai and boasting about her fertility while Sarai remained barren. She annoyed Sarai so much that Sarai fought back, and Sarai's abuse ran Hagar off into the desert. There, beside a spring, an angel came to Hagar and told her she should go back to Sarai and to Abram. The child in Hagar's womb would be strong—a fighter—and she should name him Ishmael.

This was not the child God promised Abram. This child was Abram's own answer to the promise of God. This child was the result of a grasp for significance rather than an open-handed surrender. Abram was eighty-six years old when Ishmael was born.

But God is God, and he is faithful regarding the promises he speaks over us and into us. So Abram was ninety-nine when God reached out again with an affirmation of that original promise. Can you imagine? In *The Message* version of the Bible, Abram's response to God's reaffirmation reads like this: "Overwhelmed, Abram fell flat on his face" (Gen. 17:3). Surrender looks a lot like that. We are overwhelmed, and we are not strategizing or fighting back or suggesting an alternate route. We have nothing left to do but to let God be God.

Indeed, God gave Abram and Sarai a son, and they named him Isaac, and God renamed Abram and Sarai and called them Abraham (meaning "father of many nations") and Sarah. Abraham was ninety-nine and Sarah ninety years old when this happened. Even so, God was not finished with them.

A few years after Isaac was born, God spoke to Abraham and told him to take Isaac and offer him to God as a sacrifice. And do you know what the astounding thing is? Abraham did what God told him to do. This was no thoughtless action of a brainwashed has-been. This was the result of a man having walked with God through one encounter after the other and having seen God prove himself worthy of complete trust. When Abraham agreed to offer Isaac as a sacrifice to God, he was choosing God, and surrender to God, over significance. The promise God had extended to Abraham all those years before held within it what might easily be misconstrued as significance. Being named by God as the "father of many nations" held with it great potential for the wielding of power and the benefit of popular opinion and maybe a hint of celebrity. Isaac was the promise fulfilled, and now God was telling Abraham to let it go.

We either want God or we want significance. This is the crux of the matter.

Over the years between that moment when God first gave Abraham the promise and the moment God asked Abraham to sacrifice Isaac as an offering to God, Abraham had come to find that our significance actually arrives through the surrendering of significance. Abraham had tried it his own way, and while the results *looked* like what God intended, it also brought a lot of grief in Abraham's household—grief between Hagar and Sarah, to be sure, but also grief that extends through the generations. Back at that spring in the desert, where the angel of God caught up with Hagar and convinced her to return to Abraham and Sarah, this is what the angel told Hagar:

> "Go back to your mistress. Put up with her abuse." He continued, "I'm going to give you a big family, children past counting.
>
> From this pregnancy, you'll get a son: Name him Ishmael;
> for GOD heard you, GOD answered you." (Gen. 16:9–11)

109

Then the angel continued with these words about Ishmael: "He'll be a bucking bronco of a man, a real fighter, fighting and being fought, always stirring up trouble, always at odds with his family" (Gen. 16:12).

When we search for significance outside of surrender to God, we create our own version of God's plan for us, and it rarely measures up.

As the story goes, Abraham took Isaac to the land of Moriah, just as God had commanded him. All these centuries later, I can hardly believe it when I read the words. I can feel the roughness of the rope Abraham used to tie up Isaac, and I can feel the logs beneath Isaac's back as he lay on top of the altar as the sacrifice. It is a horrific scene to imagine. There is no record that Isaac fought or struggled. There is no account of him crying out and asking his father to reconsider.

It's enough to make anyone question the goodness of this God who says he is love. Abraham reaches for the knife, and I hold my breath.

But, remember? God is always reaching for us. He is. God calls to Abraham and tells him to release the child. "Don't lay a hand on that boy! Don't touch him!" God says. "Now I know how fearlessly you fear God; you didn't hesitate to place your son, your dear son, on the altar for me" (Gen. 22:12). Then God provided a ram. There in the brush, its horns all tangled up in the thick of things, was a ram for the sacrifice.

Abraham released Isaac and sacrificed the ram instead. And Abraham named that place on that mountain Jehovah-Jireh, which means, "The Lord Provides."

God has been our provider since the very beginning. The very first gift God gives us at the very beginning of the story is breath. But there is more. Through forty-two generations, God writes a new chapter in the story. Because, when Jesus delivered us, by his death and resurrection, into new life, the first thing he gave us was breath. It showed up without warning, as the disciples huddled together at the Feast of Pentecost. All of sudden, into their wondering and grief and emptiness, there was the sound of something like a mighty, rushing wind, and the Holy Spirit was on the move, infusing the disciples with life and power and hope. The Holy Spirit is the significance we hunger for. Wait for it. Welcome it. Expect it. Surrender unto surrender and find significance in him. Open hands. Palms toward the heavens.

There is no need for building ladders to the sky or jumping through hoops to be noticed by God. The path to a life of significance leads to a dead end without the breath of the Holy Spirit to infuse us with the character and the image of an almighty and everlasting God. This is the God who loved us before we first gasped for air.

Let's be careful, though, lest we cast the Holy Spirit in the role of bargaining chip. We're not making deals with God when we release our lives into his hands. This is not a "God, if I do this for you, then you do this for me" exchange. We either want significance or we want God. It really does come down to that. If we knew it meant we'd live a life that no one noticed, or cared about, or approved of, or remarked about, or paid attention to, would we still choose God? If it meant we'd lose everything, would God still be first on our list?

Oswald Chambers puts it like this: "As long as you maintain your own personal interests and ambitions, you cannot be completely aligned or identified with God's interests. This can only be accomplished by giving up all of your personal

111

plans once and for all, and by allowing God to take you directly into His purpose for the world."[2]

This is surrender, as powerful as the air we breathe. When we choose Jesus, we choose to surrender all, freely and of our own accord. We either want significance or we want God. We cannot seek significance and find it anywhere else but in God. Everything else is breathlessness. Solomon, in the book of Ecclesiastes, calls this striving for significance without surrendering first to God "a chasing after wind" (1:14 NIV), and I don't know if he knew just how right those words are. Because what we are chasing is the fresh wind of the Holy Spirit in our lives, breathing purpose into our next gasp for air.

In the beginning, God breathed into humanity, and humanity became a living soul.

Surrender to the work of the Holy Spirit and you will come alive. Exhale, and you will live. When you have spent it all and left it on the track, when you are wrapped in silence and someone else runs all the red lights on your behalf, when you are at the end of yourself and you can barely remember the difference between up and down, choose to breathe. It is our direct reminder of the Holy Spirit at work in this world and on our behalf. It is our immediate reminder that God is always reaching toward us and lifting us to himself to breathe life into our long reach for a life that matters for something.

Breathe.

God will meet you there and receive your one, beautiful, miraculous breath as an act of worship and as a surrender of yourself into his purpose for your life.

6

Pay Attention

First, is the danger of futility; the belief there is nothing one man or one woman can do against the enormous array of the world's ills—against misery and ignorance, injustice and violence. Yet many of the world's great movements, of thought and action, have flowed from the work of a single man.

Robert F. Kennedy

One of the richest traditions in the black church is what is known as call and response. When the preacher preaches, it is not one-way communication. Preaching, in the black church tradition, is a beautiful dance between the pulpit and the pew with the Holy Spirit orchestrating the sacred exchange. The preacher makes a point, or reads a Scripture, or reminds the congregation that God is good, and the congregation responds with clapping and shouting and foot stomping and words lifted in prayerful agreement. Words like "Amen!" or "Hallelujah!" or "Thank you, Jesus!" or "Say that!" or "PREACH!" bounce around the sanctuary, and the service feels like a celebration.

This is what faith looks like: call and response. When God calls, we respond. Much is made of the saying that God answers prayer in one of three ways: yes, no, or not yet. The same is true of our answers back to God when he speaks to us. We, created with free will, have the very same options at our disposal. God does not twist our arm until we bow in submission. God lets us choose. He calls us to himself, and he is patient as we sort through all the facts. But the choice is ours. We can respond to God with yes, no, or not yet. Our response is predicated on so many things, including our level of trust in God, our willingness to surrender to God, and our general comfort level. Of course, what God always desires from us is our yes. But he's not pushy. When God extends the invitation, we either trust him or we don't. When we choose to trust him even though the thought terrifies us, he is not put off if we are shaking in our boots when we say yes. And just because we are shaking in our boots doesn't mean we don't trust God.

If you've read the book *Experiencing God* by Henry Blackaby, you are familiar with the idea that God is always at work around us, that we should look to see where God is at work and join him there, and that God in fact invites us to join him. It's one of the craziest things, isn't it?

God doesn't need my help in this world any more than you or I need our toddlers to help us make the bed, or mix up the brownies, or fold the laundry. In fact, asking our children to help often means the job will take longer and require us to tidy things up when the tiny fingers have moved on to digging in the dirt and building LEGO castles. But we delight in them and we desire to teach them, so we invite them along for the ride.

God delights in us, and he has asked us to be his hands and feet here in the world. He doesn't need us, but he has chosen to work out his will through us.

We look around at our world today and wonder, *Who will be our Dr. King or Gandhi or Mother Teresa or Nelson Mandela?* and we forget that God is always doing something new. God isn't looking for the next King or Gandhi or Mother Teresa or Nelson Mandela. God is extending a hand in your direction, hoping you'll join him. When you say yes, God works in you and through you to bring about significant and lasting change for good and for the kingdom. God wants to do a new thing in our world and in our time. Chances are good that you are the perfect person for the job.

But we want to be sure. We want to know we are on the right track. Many of us don't balk at the idea of surrender, as long as we know that in the end, it will have all been worth it. We want to be convinced we're hearing right and that God is truly on our side and leading the charge.

This is nothing new. We are not the first generation of people to second-guess God's call to us. The biblical account of Gideon and God's call to him is a perfect example of this second-guessing and requests of God for proof (see Judg. 6).

When God showed up on Gideon's doorstep, calling Gideon a mighty warrior and commissioning Gideon to save Israel from the Midianites, Gideon was not immediately persuaded. The angel of God proclaimed that God was with Gideon, and Gideon looked around him and wasn't convinced he was hearing right. What Gideon saw before him did not square up with what the angel of God was saying. As Gideon saw it, the people of God were at the mercy of the Midianites, subject to terrible poverty and hunger, and diminished to cowering in caves, out of sight of their enemy. So when God showed up on the scene to tell Gideon he was with Gideon and present with his people, Gideon wasn't such an easy sell.

"If God is with us, why has all this happened to us? Where are all the miracle-wonders our parents and grandparents told us about, telling us, 'Didn't GOD deliver us from Egypt?' The fact is, God has nothing to do with us—he has turned us over to Midian" (Judg. 6:13). This was Gideon's boldly frustrated reply to the messenger of God.

As it turns out, not only was God with Gideon, but God had chosen Gideon to lead the defeat of the Midianites.

After a bit of back-and-forth between Gideon and God, Gideon relented just a bit. Gideon said, "If you're serious about this, do me a favor: Give me a sign to back up what you're telling me. Don't leave until I come back and bring you my gift" (Judg. 6:17).

Ah, the signs. Talk about signs in the Bible, and someone will eventually turn to Gideon. He was a master. Gideon asked God for a sign at that first meeting between him and God, and God obliged Gideon by breaking fire forth from a rock with the tip of a stick in his hand. Convinced God had his back, but under cover of night, Gideon gathered ten men and tore down his father's Baal altar and fertility pole, both of which were symbols of idol worship and a turning away from God.

Emboldened by that experience, Gideon went across the river, set up camp, and called for warriors who might join him in this battle against the Midianites to which God was calling him. But just to be sure he was on the right track, Gideon asked God for another sign that Gideon was headed in the right direction.

> Gideon said to God, "If this is right, if you are using me to save Israel as you've said, then look: I'm placing a fleece of wool on the threshing floor. If dew is on the fleece only, but the floor is dry, then I know that you will use me to save Israel, as you said."
>
> That's what happened. When he got up early the next morning, he wrung out the fleece—enough dew to fill a bowl with water!
>
> Then Gideon said to God, "Don't be impatient with me, but let me say one more thing. I want to try another time with the fleece. But this time let the fleece stay dry, while dew drenches the ground."
>
> God made it happen that very night. Only the fleece was dry while the ground was wet with dew. (Judg. 6:36–39)

If Gideon's need for assurance and then reassurance sounds like conversations you have with God, you are not alone. It's normal to want to question if what we're hearing is actually from God or if it's from some weary and wishful place in our own mind. These are the moves we make—all the things that happen before we agree with God that we're in. We are much like Gideon, stalling for time, asking God to wait while he slaughters a bull and prepares an offering. And then all of those fleeces! Sign upon sign. Hoping God might change his mind, or see the truth that Gideon wasn't really the person for the job.

That I'm not the person for the job!

It's okay to go through the process. Even Jesus, in the New Testament, cautions us to consider the cost. Just be sure to realize the process is about me, and about you, and not at all about God. When God calls to us, he's already got everything worked out. We're the ones who get distracted by all the checking of the ducks and the rows in which they may or may not seem to be standing. The call is sent forth, but there is no response because we've gotten all tangled up in the details and the multiple requests for multiple signs. There comes a point where our counting the cost crosses over into something less constructive.

Much to our disappointment, we don't get to see the entire story before it unfolds. If it were up to me, God would drop down a neon sign from heaven with detailed instructions about where we were headed next and why, how long it would take us to get there, and who we might encounter along the way. But that's not usually how it goes, is it? We are simply called to walk through the doors that open in front of us. We are asked to wait when no doors open. We are advised to resist the urge to knock down the doors that have been padlocked and sealed shut to us. It is a tentative dance we find ourselves in, requiring us to listen more than we speak and to wait more than we'd like.

Years ago, when my husband and I were contemplating an important move, we invited a wise and trusted adviser to join us as we traveled to the new city for a weekend of interviews and conversation and prayerful consideration. While we were there, my husband and I both were enthralled by the city and by the people who welcomed us warmly, and we could picture ourselves packing up our things and moving our lives to this new placc. But beneath the current of enthusiasm rested an uncertain little nudge that kept rising to the surface over the course of our weekend there. As the three of us walked along the way or sat across from each other in coffee shops, or when we checked in with each other at the end of the day, our trusted adviser wisely advised my husband and me with two simple words. "Pay attention," he'd say to us. In the end, we didn't make that move. The door was shut to us, and we knew not to press against it.

Those two words have become a mantra in our family: *Pay attention.*

When something keeps rising to the top in your life, pay attention to it. Even if it seems like nothing much at all. It may seem like just a little thing, but if it keeps surfacing, pay attention to it. When questions continue to nudge you, pay attention to them. When you keep looking at a particular situation and you wonder where is the next Martin Luther King Jr. or Mother Teresa or Nelson Mandela, pay attention, because chances are good that God is hand-delivering an invitation and that particular invitation is embossed with your name on it.

Our adviser's wise words in that particular situation led us to see that God wasn't opening a door for us there. But we continue to heed our adviser's advice and pay attention. When we do, we have also seen God standing at doors which have swung wide open, his foot in the jamb, holding the doors open before us and saying, "This is the way. Walk in it."

Perhaps you've begun to feel a stirring in your gut that has nothing to do with the pizza you ate last night and everything to do with the next step God may be calling you to take.

You can't be sure what's around the bend. You doubt the difference your one life can make in such a massive universe.

You're not even sure you know the first step to take, and if you took it, you're not sure if it would be because of the Holy Spirit or because you've lost your mind.

I feel you.

Robert F. Kennedy said in a farewell speech given in Warsaw, Poland, and reported in the *New York Times* in 1964, "Just because we cannot see clearly the end of the road, that is no reason for not setting out on this most essential journey."[1]

When someone moves forward in faith and takes that first step, onlookers call it brave, but it only looks that way from the outside. If it were only brave, it would be something other than faith. Brave by itself is something we work up on our own, and it allows us to point at ourselves and at our accomplishment and say, "Look what I did!"

Faith is when you say yes to God with no courage in sight. Faith leads us to brave.

It is faith that causes us to accept the invitation God hands to us, even when it scares us. No one ever said it has to be huge faith. Jesus himself said that faith the size of a little mustard seed is enough to move mountains (see Matt. 17:20).

God is not nearly as concerned with our comfort as he is with our character. So he invites us over the edge and outside our comfort zones. Ask Moses and Nehemiah. Sit for a while with our friend Gideon, who kept making God prove to him that God really intended Gideon to lead an army of only three hundred men. Ask Esther, who knew she might lose her very life if she spoke truth to power. Spend some time with Hagar or Jael or Mary, the mother of Jesus.

On my website I often host conversations about race, culture, ethnicity, and diversity in the North American church. It's not a conversation I sought to host. In fact, I tried to get out of it. I've tried to exit the conversation a few times. But it began—and continues—as a natural response to a question I started asking so many decades ago: "Why can't the church figure out how to worship across lines of race, ethnicity, and culture?"

For a few years each October, Myquillyn Smith, aka The Nester, invited readers to write for thirty days about one topic and to post those daily entries on their own websites. The first year I participated, my husband and I had just sold a big house and a lot of our stuff and had moved to a tiny rental just a few blocks away. I decided I'd write for thirty days that year about living small. It was a good discipline for me as a writer, and the following year, when the thirty-day challenge started to approach again, I wondered what topic to choose. Instantly, the idea to write Thirty Days in My Brown Skin came to mind.

Whoa. I sat with the idea for a bit. It was risky. It was dangerous. It had the potential to go wrong in so many ways. I had quiet conversations about it with God. I had multiple conversations about it with my husband and with a couple of friends who have their own websites. I considered the risks, and they were many. But I also considered the possibility a project like this had to inject a small bit of grace into a conversation that might be tough and frustrating and that, as far as I could tell, often got stalled more times than it got started. I was putting out fleeces. And God was patient with me. He waited while I explored the possibilities and asked my questions and slowly became convinced the series was the right thing to do. All I had to go on was a question that had been nagging me for decades and an open door in front of me.

I was not brave.

I reached out to a friend of mine—a white woman with one biological daughter and one adopted daughter who is black. I told this friend I planned to write a series called Thirty Days in My Brown Skin, and I asked if she'd consider writing a guest entry on the topic of race in America, as the adoptive mother of a black child. She agreed right away—another open door. But a few days after she said yes, I doubted. I second-guessed. I made a unilateral decision to chuck the idea. "No one wants to read about race," I thought to myself. "Why open that can of worms?" I asked myself. And so I decided to skip the thirty-day writing challenge that year.

But God is persistent.

Just a few days before the thirty-day challenge was scheduled to begin, I happened to be reading a few updates on Twitter. While reading, I happened upon an announcement from the friend I'd asked to write about race as a guest on my site. Her announcement said something like, "So excited! A black woman writing for 30 days about race in America!" In this Twitter announcement, my friend included a web link to this black woman's website.

"Cool!" I thought to myself. I clicked on the link, planning to bookmark this woman's site and follow her for the entire thirty days. "Thank you, God," I prayed as the page on my laptop loaded. "Thank you for calling a black woman to write on this topic." And there on my screen right in front of my eyes was my head shot!

I'd never told my friend I had backed out. I never told her I wasn't going to write about race after all. So there it was—an announcement to her followers that I (me!) would indeed be writing for thirty days about race.

Gulp!

There was no turning back.

I was not brave, and the situation required me to lean hard on faith. There was no time for fleeces or for second-guessing. All that was left to do was to take the next step.

Please don't take this as me saying God will announce your next step to you on social media, or that he will boss you around and "make you" do something. That's not the way God operates. The way this unfolded was a perfect fit for me. I enjoy social media, and I was already committed to the idea of race and the church, but I didn't really know where to go with it. God used what worked for me to gently point me back to the path.

Before God extends an invitation to you, he has already been getting you ready for it. It may not seem like it in the moment, but God does not suddenly get an idea and then grab the first person he sees passing by. No, God is at work outside of time, and he chooses a path for us for which we are uniquely suited. Gideon's response to God in the Old Testament book of Judges attests to this.

I imagine Gideon in the winepress before God showed up and commissioned him for the battle against the Midianites. Gideon knew the stories of this great God who delivered his people out of slavery in Egypt. He must have been rehearsing these stories in his head as he threshed out the wheat in the winepress, out of sight of his enemy. He recounted in his mind the stories of miracles and wonders that he'd heard his parents and grandparents tell over the years. And he couldn't reconcile it in his mind.

This great God had worked so specifically and succinctly in the lives of the people of Israel, but in Gideon's case, up to that moment, it seemed this God was nowhere to be found.

And so when God announced himself to Gideon, Gideon presented an argument in two parts:

1. God is not with us. God has turned us over to Midian.
2. I am not the person for this job. My clan is the weakest, and I am the runt of the litter.

These two premises were the result of a long line of questioning that I imagine Gideon must have sorted through during his days of hiding out in the winepress. His questions may have sounded like this: "Where is this great God my parents told me about? If God is so great, why are we at the mercy of our enemy? Why are we hiding? Who will save us? Who will rescue us? Where is our Moses? Who will be our Joshua?"

Sound familiar?

God showed up with answers Gideon wasn't ready to believe:

1. I am with you.
2. I am sending you, Gideon. Not Moses or Joshua. You. You are the person for this job.

What if God is saying the same thing to you today? *I am with you. You are the person for this job.*

There is only one way to tell if the question that keeps bugging you or the calling you think you hear is from God or from some crooked place in your head. Go ahead and test the question against the Word of God. Run it by your closest friends. Take it to a trusted pastor or spiritual adviser and see if he or she gives you a look of concern. Pray. Pay attention. But the only way to know for sure, after you've done all you know to do and the invitation still stands, is to say yes—walk through the door that opens before you, and see what happens.

Part 3

Taking the Next Step

7

The Gospel Needs to Be Lived

To be a Christian who is willing to travel with Christ on his downward road requires being willing to detach oneself constantly from any need to be relevant, and to trust ever more deeply the Word of God.

Henri Nouwen

What does it matter that God so loved the world? Do you ever wonder that? Do you ever sit and question whether it is really true or whether, by choosing Jesus over all else, you've been duped? What if we get to the end of this life and discover it was all a farce? What if we die and find out heaven is not for real and God is nowhere to be found and love does not, in fact, cover a multitude of sins? What if we've chosen wrong?

What if we've believed the wrong thing? What if the people with the picket signs were right, after all?

Aren't these the unspeakable questions? Aren't these the questions that keep our minds spinning in a downward spiral in the earliest hours of the day and the solitary hours in the darkness of the night? What if the gospel is a myth concocted by terrified human beings who feel desperately small and helpless and who need something to cling to in order to make it through life on this crumbling, spinning, lonely planet that holds us captive by the force of gravity and dares us to break free?

Some days it is easy to lose sight of the gospel.

Our church isn't one of the fancy ones. Not on the surface. We don't have a groovy stage or a slick order of worship. Most Sundays someone chimes in from the congregation with something like, "Hey, are you going to have an offering today?" or "There's no potluck this weekend. It's next week." Sometimes in the winter the furnace fails and keeps us wrapped in our coats through the service, and sometimes in the summer the air conditioner breaks, leading us to open up the doors wide and hold our arms so that our elbows don't touch our bodies while we fan ourselves with our printed bulletins. Often, those of us in the congregation cringe politely as the guys in the sound booth try to eliminate the squealing feedback from one of the singers' microphones.

Always, it is a beautiful sight to behold: all of this ordinary humanity, stumbling through the order of worship in every little bit of our regular-ness. We expect to experience God, or we don't, or wc simply have no other place to send ourselves on Sunday mornings, and so this is where we end up. But we are no mystery to God. We never stump him. Somehow we bring him with us, and he also meets us there, and then he leaves with us and joins us for lunch, and having been there changes us, even if we don't realize it yet.

I've been married to a minister long enough to know that everyone in ministry has moments of insecurity. We can't help it, because we are human and every now and then, humans get insecure. Ministers, pastors, worship leaders, youth workers—pick your church worker—all of them are human. Ministers and pastors and the people they marry and the children they raise are not privy to any greater access to God than anyone else. And ministers and pastors and the people they marry and the children they raise are no less susceptible to all of the things that trip up the rest of the human race. You don't have to look too far to find a story of a minister who has missed the mark in some way. Everything, from the smallest miscalculation to the grossest and most base transgression, has befallen people who wear the title "minister."

We had little children and had just bought our first house when Harry one day said to God, "Why can't my ministry be big like so-and-so's? Why can't I be one of the rich and famous?" Harry tells me God spoke to him right away that day. God said, "No one is immune to corruption." We are not immune. Because, well, like everyone else, these people who work in churches are human.

From time to time, pastors compare their ministries to other pastors' ministries, the same way the rest of us compare shoes and cars and the behavior of our children and our success in the vocation to which we feel called. I'm not saying it's right. I'm just saying it is something that happens. And there is always someone with a bigger congregation, a more successful youth ministry, a more powerful missionary ministry, a more rocking praise band or gospel choir, or a more skilled graphic designer. Someone else out there will always preach a better message or be invited on the latest talk show or get picked up by a bigger publisher.

I think sometimes our insecurities get the best of us. I think we get caught up in wishing we had someone else's calling, and we forget the reason we set out on this particular path in the first place. I think these are some of the reasons that when we are not careful, it's sometimes easy to lose sight of the gospel.

One Saturday, while riding our bikes around town in the evening before church the following morning, Harry asked me, "What is the gospel?"

Every now and then, my husband asks me questions like these. They are questions that surprise me, because, you know, I think a pastor should know the answers to questions such as these. We spent a boatload of money on seminary, and he's been at this ministry thing for decades, and he unpacks Scripture in ways that make my faith grow leaps and bounds in one sitting. Yet sometimes, over my shoulder, as we ride our bikes beneath the oak trees, I'll hear something from his lips that sounds exactly like a human being trying to figure things out. "What is the gospel?"

Of course, when questions like these come up, my mind is elsewhere. It is writing grocery lists or singing the chorus of "I Will Survive" or trying to remember whether I switched the linens from the washer to the dryer before we left the house that afternoon. In other words, I am caught off guard and I might tend toward pithy and trite, or depending on the weather, I might try a little bit of humor. On this particular summer evening, while I shifted gears to match the incline on the bike trail, I turned my head to the left so my voice would reach him over my shoulder, and I said, "It's the Good News!" as if he'd forgotten.

"But what's the Good News?" he asked me.

I was not prepared for this response. Surely I had nailed it with my first answer. So I tried again: "For God so loved the world . . ."

"Yeah, yeah, yeah," he said. "But so what?" Later he would tell me, "I don't know if this ministry thing is for me anymore."

He is human. Pastor or not, he is just like the rest of us who wake up one morning and suddenly wonder if we've chosen the wrong path, picked the wrong major, focused on the wrong thing, missed the mark, heard wrong, or just plain used up all of our options, and now we find ourselves standing at the door to the future with our pockets emptied and turned inside out.

"What are you saying?" I asked him.

"I don't know," he said to me. "I just don't think I've got what it takes these days. I don't think I do a very good job of making the gospel relevant." He was not asking for my pity or my sympathy. I knew this. He was having a moment. "There are so many others out there," he said, "who do this so much better than me."

If you haven't had one of these moments yourself, just keep on living (as my grandmother used to say). Your moment is coming. You can count on it. If you haven't already, one day you will stumble upon someone who does something or has something or says something or creates something or performs something better than you can or have or ever will. And the thing that makes it worse is simply knowing they have what they have or do what they do because of the very

131

same Jesus you've said you were going to follow. So why, you wonder to yourself, is that person getting all the attention, and what do you have to do in order to be as successful as her?

Let me warn you right here and now, and let me be clear when I say it: it is a dangerous thing to think we can measure the impact of the gospel in our lives against the impact of that very same gospel in someone else's life. It is a sneaky trick and a lie to believe that God intends for us to compete against one another or to compare ourselves to others. We are admonished to consider the work of our hands as an offering to the Lord.

Neither our work nor our lives are put on display to receive accolades and awards and the approval of people. If we are listening, we hear or we think we hear the voice of God, and we do our best to follow his leading and to say yes to his invitation, even though our hearts faint within us. We respond to his voice as an act of worship, and we leave our offering—the cutting of a grilled cheese sandwich for a hungry toddler, the submission of a quarterly sales report to our employer, the paying of taxes, the delivery of a sermon, the hours sitting quietly beside a hospital bed, the singing of a hymn, the washing of a dish, the pulling of weeds, the giving of a monetary gift, the knitting of a shawl, and all the other beautifully ordinary gifts of an average day—at his feet. No matter where you live out your calling, whether in your home with three rambunctious toddlers or in an arena of tens of thousands, the act of worship is intimate and personal. Because of the gospel—the Good News—we enter into the Holy of Holies, behind the veil. It is no small thing.

In the Old Testament, the priest who entered the Holy of Holies to present an offering on behalf of the people had

132

a cord tied around his ankle so that, should the priest be overcome by either the intimacy or the wrath of God, those standing outside without the clearance to enter could pull out the priest's body by grabbing hold of the cord. We don't step into a fairy tale when we choose to live out the gospel.

Whether we respond to the call of God by extending kindness to our difficult neighbor or by traveling over the ocean to speak to thousands of conference attendees, the act of living out the gospel as a response to the invitation and call of God is intimate and not to be compared with anyone else's act of worship.

The word worship means "to ascribe worth to someone or something." When we worship something or someone, we lift up its value as being worthy of honor. But what if, without intending to, we end up skewing the object of our worship so that it is our calling or our success or our way of doing things or even ourselves we end up lauding, above the God who deserves our highest hallelujahs?

It is no accident, nor is it an editorial oversight, that Paul tells us marriage is a model of Christ and the church. As the body of Christ, we are considered the bride of Christ, and each one of us, individually, is invited to an intimate relationship with our Lord, a personal relationship that rivals even the most wonderful earthly marriage.

God loves us. God loves you. This, my friend, is the gospel. The relevant Good News.

God loved us enough to send his Son to live and move among us. Jesus Christ, the Word of God made flesh, walked the earth and ministered to the lost and lonely and to the high and mighty. He was put to death on a cross, and your sins and mine were nailed up there with him, and our sins died there with him when he breathed his last. He was dead, and he was buried in a borrowed tomb, and in an astoundingly miraculous event, he rose to life again. Now Jesus sits at the right hand of God, talking to God on our behalf. But Jesus did not leave us alone when he rose from death to heaven. Now we have access to the Holy Spirit, who teaches us all things and reminds us of everything Jesus did and said and was while he walked the dusty roads and calmed the seas and gave sight to the blind. The Holy Spirit interprets the cries of our fainting hearts to the Father, and God extends an invitation to us to receive it all. We, in turn, find ourselves in love with God and extending this love from God to everyone around us.

This, oh lovely one, is the salty, savory, succulent Good News, and there is no need to pretty it up or to infuse it with anything fancy like strategies and target demographics and spreadsheets and programs and building projects and light shows and five-part harmonies. The gospel of Jesus Christ stands on its own. Our desire to offer up worship experiences and mission trips and Sunday morning services that run smoothly and that create beauty should rise up in us, deeply rooted in love, as a response to this gospel—this Good News.

These acts of worship are not the Good News but rather a response to the Good News. Without the gospel of Jesus Christ as the very foundation on which they are built, they will fail to do anything more than point to themselves or to the people who administer them. Our acts of worship as we live out the gospel in our everyday lives are like gentle reminders, one after the other, ascribing worth to God and inviting the world to consider Jesus in every little thing. We don't need to work things up or measure our performance against our neighbor's or against some crazy mark of perfec-

134

tion we think we need to obtain. We simply live our lives as the person God created us to be (introvert, extrovert, tall, short, brown, beige, male, female, etc.) and in the role of our current season of life (spouse, parent, child, employee, employer, retiree, volunteer, community member, neighbor, etc.), mindful of the Good News and in awe of Jesus.

Jesus Christ is so very attractive. The Bible tells us things that lead us to believe he may not have been so easy on the eyes, but that does not belie the truth of his attractiveness. He is winsome, and we realize this when we turn our eyes in his direction. It is when our eyes wander that we forget the powerful truth of the salty Good News.

"You are the salt of the earth" (Matt. 5:13 NIV).

Sometimes what we need is a reminder that the gospel is more than enough. It is ruddy and rustic, and it defies logic, and we wonder if it can stand on its own after all.

There is nothing we need to add to or subtract from the gospel. We can't make it be what it isn't. We cannot twist it to mean something it was never meant to mean.

We blame a lot of stuff on God that had nothing at all to do with him. We take liberty with his name and his power, and we ascribe to him the approval of unspeakable things. Things like slavery and genocide and picketing outside funerals and pointing fingers and choosing sides and isms of every stripe. This is not the gospel. This is not Good News.

The gospel, in its very basic form, gives us all the direction we need. Love God, and then love people the same way you love yourself. Because we are individuals, each with unique and intimate relationships with God, the gospel gets lived out through us in many different ways, in response to what the gospel calls out of us.

These days, however, I hardly ever hear anyone talking about feeling "called by God" to enter into ministry, or into any other vocation, for that matter. In fact, saying you feel called, or that God spoke to you about such and such a thing, is more likely to gain questioning looks than nods of affirmation, even from those in the church. Or maybe I'm simply not hanging out around the right people anymore.

But let me ask you something: If God is real and alive, like we so often claim he is, and if he spoke the world into existence, and if he desires an intimate relationship with us as we say he does and as the Bible tells us, and if God loved us enough to send his Son to us and then told us the story of this great gift by saying, "The Word became flesh . . ." (John 1:14 NIV), then why wouldn't God speak? To us? Today?

Perhaps people have gotten quiet about hearing from God because in claiming to hear from God, so many of us have tried to lay claim to God. We've heard pastors call their churches Holy Ghost headquarters, as if the Holy Spirit could be contained in one infinitesimally small church building here on this speck of dust we call Earth. And let's face it: no matter how large the church building or congregation, no matter how popular the writer or how broad the reach of her ministry, it is all still so very infinitesimally small when compared to the God of the universe.

Maybe people have grown justifiably weary of hearing people invoke the holy name of God in order to twist the truth and solidify their own power and position. When we say we've heard from God and then twist the truth to our own advantage and glory, we have forgotten the part about God being a jealous God, a God who rightfully desires all the praise and honor and glory to go to him. The Bible calls this working of things to our own advantage vainglory, which, when translated from the Greek, means "empty pride."

So I get it. I understand why people may shy away from saying they've heard from God. It can leave a bad taste in the mouth. And isn't that one way to tell truth from fiction, or from myth?

> Open your mouth and taste, open your eyes and see —
> how good GOD is.
> Blessed are you who run to him.
>
> Psalm 34:8

God is good, and his words are sweet medicine to the soul. I'm not talking about good as in, "if you choose to follow him you will win the lottery and you'll never get sick or be fired or break up with your loved one or experience abuse or persecution or death." The gospel is not a feel-good message, designed to lull us into complacency and groupthink. But neither is it ours to manipulate and coerce into our own agenda and game plan.

I am not a theologian. Not in the strict sense of the word. I want to know God, and I want to know about God, and I want to be known by God. I want to be in awe of him, and I want to be caught up by him, and on my best days, I desire to be absorbed into him, so much so that it's difficult for the world to tell us apart.

I am a lover of the capital *C* Church, the body of Christ. And I am a lover of the local church. But maybe what I'm thinking is that we've gotten a little too picky with our gospel. We pick at it like a loose strand of yarn on a burgundy sweater, and before we know it, the whole thing has unraveled and left us with nothing to protect us from the cold or with which to comfort the shivering soul of our neighbor, who breathes this air and trudges about on terra firma right along with us. We've picked at the gospel for so long and so hard that all we have is a ball of used-up burgundy yarn draped across our toes and tangled up around our ankles.

The other day, in a bookstore in my community, I stood in front of a bookshelf. It was filled with books, with shelves that reached a few feet above my head and spread out on either side of me. A sign at the top of this section of books labeled this part of the bookstore "Defending the Faith," and I was struck by the nature of the word *defend*. "What is the gospel?" I asked myself. I wanted to know if it is something that needs defending. Because I think what the gospel really needs is to be lived. Love the Lord your God with everything available to you—your heart, your mind, your soul, and your strength. And love your neighbor as you love yourself (see Mark 12:30–31). Some have boiled these verses down to four words in two sentences: "Love God. Love others."

It can be easy to read those four words and think they are weak or watered down. It can be easy to believe those four words don't offer enough of a challenge. But what happens when we actually begin living them? When we approach every little thing in our lives with a love for God and a love for everyone around us—even our enemies, *especially* our enemies—we swim against the current and walk against the grain. Living the Good News in every encounter is no small endeavor. In fact, when held up against one another, living the gospel is probably much more difficult than defending it. What if, instead of defending the faith, we began the hard work of loving God and loving people with everything available to us?

The gospel of Jesus is not a white-glove affair, and it is not dependent on whether we sing on key and clap our hands on two and four or on one and three. It needs to be lived more than it needs to be defended. The gospel of Jesus will stand on its own, whether we are Presbyterian or Lutheran or Anglican or Mennonite or nondenominational or American Baptist or Mormon or Muslim or Jewish or None. The gospel of Jesus is impervious to our shenanigans and our scheduled board meetings and our shunnings and our shamings and our slightings of one another. The gospel of Jesus does not need us to make it right or true, or worthy of our attention or devotion. It does not ask us to draw lines of division or to build walls of separation. It doesn't need a new wardrobe or a new method of delivery. It doesn't need to be timed or altered or picked at any more. The gospel needs to be lived.

We don't make the gospel relevant. The gospel is relevant in spite of us. The gospel of Jesus Christ was born relevant. We don't need more conferences or retreats or networks or churches or fund-raisers or missions trips or rescuers to make the gospel be what it has always been, right from the beginning of time.

This is no new-fangled thing. This incredible life-giving, world-changing mystery we call the gospel is ancient and sacred and holy. It was here long before we arrived on the scene, and when our bodies have turned to dust beneath the surface of the earth, or in the farthest reaches of the depths of the sea, or in an inferno of flames, the gospel of Jesus Christ will still be true and real and powerful and mysterious and worthy of attention and devotion.

Choosing to believe the gospel and to try to live it out is not a journey for the faint of heart. Even though that's the way we all begin, isn't it? Our hearts faint at the slightest inconvenience or disturbance, or even at the very mention of turbulence. I've said it before: Jesus doesn't tell us to count the cost for nothing.

You do not need to fancy up your life. You don't need a bigger platform, or a more significant ministry, or a bigger house, or another circle of friends, or more members in your small group, or anything more than what you have when you lift your eyes from this page and take a good, long look around you. The gospel of Jesus Christ does not need us to make it anything more than it already is. What the gospel of Jesus Christ invites us to do is to be exactly who we are, in the places where we find ourselves, and to be infused with the salty goodness that comes when we surrender our lives and our agendas and our hopes and dreams to the power and the control of the Holy Spirit.

It is no small gesture, this surrender to a gospel life. The power of the Holy Spirit will transform you first, and it will begin on the inside of your fainting heart. It will be sweet and intimate and beautiful and risky, and you will wonder if your heart can take it. But go with it. Release your grip. Give the performance a rest, and let him in. God is not going to force himself on you. He is persistent, and that is because of the unsearchable love he has for you. He holds a torch for your heart, but he waits patiently for you to respond to his gentle advances. He will not give up. He will not give in. He will not place a checklist in front of you or require you to get your act together. He will leave the choice up to you, because who wants to have someone love them out of a sense of obligation? God is not needy like that. God is sure of his love and devotion toward you, and God is equally sure that he is worthy of your heart.

☆ ⭐ ☆ ☆ ★ ★ *8* ☆ ☆ ☆ ⭐ ★ ☆ ⭐

Every Little Thing

Some believe it is only great power that can hold evil in check. But that is not what I have found. I have found that it is the small everyday deeds of ordinary folks that keep the darkness at bay. Small acts of kindness and love.

J. R. R. Tolkien, *The Hobbit*

I have always been small. I was always the line leader in school. Not because of my great leadership abilities but because of my stature. We lined up from shortest to tallest, and when it was time to take group photos—the ones where risers were set up in the gym and we were arranged around a small, rectangular black sign with plastic white letters that told our teacher's name, our grade, and the name of our school—I was always right there in the front row, grinning, with my pigtails sticking straight out from my head at awkward angles.

Small served me well for many years. It made me cute and approachable, and in some peoples' minds, it even made me sweet. But somewhere along the way, small started to feel like a weakness.

"Vertically challenged," some people said. My shoulders slumped when I heard it, so I learned to stand with my feet planted solidly beneath me, taking up as much space as I could when talking with administrators and CEOs and people with power and shoppers who could reach up and get something off the top shelf for me in the grocery store.

Small started to feel needy and helpless and insignificant and invisible. It was a lot of work, always trying to be bigger than I am and trying to fill up space that was out of my reach. I have grown as tall as I'm ever going to be. In fact, before too long, I may begin to lose ground in the stature game. Gravity has been having its way with me for more than five decades, and I am not made for this forever. Not on this side of the veil. This life I live, the lives we all live, are temporary and they are finite, and when we measure out our years against the backdrop of all that has been and all that is yet to come, no matter how tall we stand in these physical bodies that our souls inhabit for this season, we are small, all of us. What if that's okay?

I had to find my way back to feeling good about small. And I did. I grew into my smallness. It was me. It *is* me. In fact, I hardly notice it, until I find myself in a sea of big.

Nebraska is big.

When I first moved to Nebraska from the East Coast, I could not get over the vastness of the sky. Everywhere I looked,

142

there was sky. One afternoon during my lunch break at work, I buckled myself into the driver's seat of my car and started driving west. I had lived in Lincoln for a little more than a year, and in all that time I still had not been able to reconcile myself to the idea that the Great Plains rolled on and on without interruption for hundred and hundreds of miles. Lincoln is the capital city of Nebraska, but there is no cluster of skyscrapers here, towering above a bustling city of high-heeled CEOs and graffiti-adorned facades. The tallest building is the state capitol at fifteen stories high. Everywhere I went in those first months of life in Nebraska, it seemed the sky watched me, fanning out about my head in a way that felt strangely heavy and oppressive.

There was no place to hide. There was nowhere to get away from the great expanse of space and its constant reminder that I was exposed and vulnerable beneath its gaze. Some nights, when I had to head north to Omaha to pick up my husband at the airport, driving between Lincoln and Omaha on the long, flat, straight stretch of Interstate 80, I felt suffocated by the never-ending darkness, which offered no respite beyond the tunnel vision of the headlights of my car.

I needed skyscrapers or tall pine trees standing straight and breaking up the expanse of space. I needed stately evergreens growing right up to the edge of the road, just like on the Merritt Parkway where I used to drive from New York City to Connecticut when we lived back east.

So one afternoon I drove my car for miles and miles, believing there would surely be a city with skyscrapers or a stretch of highway with tall pine trees. But through the windshield of my little Honda Civic, all I saw in every direction, for miles and miles, was sky.

143

It seemed crazy to me that I would feel cramped and stifled and stunted and squelched by so much openness and fresh air and sunshine and billowy clouds. I was no match for so much vastness. I couldn't fill up the space or plant my feet in such a way to make myself seem bigger, no matter how I tried. No one could reach up to the top shelf on my behalf, and so, over time, I gave in to the sky and it became my confidant.

Have you experienced this—feeling cramped and stifled and stunted and squelched in our great big world, under the eye of a vast and billowy God? Do you look around from your small vantage point and gaze at people living large and standing squarely in their purpose, and then wonder what in the world you could possibly have to offer that might make a dent in the cosmos for good? For God? Does it terrify you? Does it bore you? Have you grown disinterested in all the hype about dreams and changing the world and making a difference right where you are?

I feel you. I hear the call right along with you. The call to let all the hoopla blow over and to simply make it from one day to the next without drawing too much attention to myself. I feel the draw of my own front stoop and the entice-ment of ordinary, and I am tempted to tender my resigna-tion in the Game of All That Is Big with a parting line that sounds something like, "If you need me, look for me where the small people play."

I am tempted to tender my resignation and then to feel ashamed for not being able to hang out or to hold my own in the big kids' playground. But I'd be using the wrong measur-ing cup, wouldn't I?

We have divided this world, and our lives in it, into card-board boxes that read *All* or *Nothing*. We think in extremes, and we experience the world as fabulous or horrendous. We are a generation of reactionaries, and we hold the feet of people we barely know to the fire, demanding *they* react a certain way, within a certain time frame, and with exactly the right words, and if they don't do it the way we think they should, we cast them aside and brush the palms of our hands together with loud, slapping sounds that we mistake for applause. We crave our news in ninety-second segments, and we also want it available twenty-four hours of every single day, and then we cower in fear at the ever-escalating reports designed to keep us tuned in by their crafty turns of phrase and the captivating skills of round-the-clock editorial teams.

We feel smaller and smaller, and we translate that to mean we have nothing to offer. We wrap our cloaks around our shoulders and step inside out of the light, shaking our heads while the screen door latches itself behind us. We convince ourselves we have nothing at all to contribute in a world that cries out for God's promise of redemption and restoration. "That's for the bigwigs," we say to ourselves. And then, "I'm no bigwig," we whisper into the darkness, our breath swirling ethereally before us in fragile wisps of fog.

In a world of hyperbolic information, I often feel an affinity toward our friend Gideon. Especially since Gideon was justified in cowering there in a cave, threshing wheat in a winepress (see Judg. 6).

It didn't really matter that God himself had told Gideon's people, and by extension God had told Gideon, "Don't for a minute be afraid" (Judg. 6:10). Gideon was, in fact, afraid. He and his people—God's chosen people—were being terrorized.

This scene depicted in Judges 6, with Gideon cowering in a winepress, threshing wheat out of sight of the Midianites, opens forty years after Deborah and Jael led the Israelites in the defeat of Sisera, his nine hundred iron chariots, and all the troops who were with him in battle. It was Jael who drove a tent stake through the temple of Sisera and into the ground beneath as he hid in her home, asleep and afraid for his life. It was Deborah, prophet and judge, who foretold the truth that God would use a woman to deliver the Israelites from the oppression imposed upon them by the hand of Sisera. With the defeat of Sisera, under the hand of the Lord, Israel enjoyed peace and restoration for forty years.

But the people of God are short of memory, it seems. What is it that causes us to forget the blessing of peace when we have tasted its delicate nectar? Why do we settle so easily into its arms and forget what it meant to be in need or to feel distress or dis-ease? I am the first to forget that peace is not a commodity to be hoarded. Nor is it a flimsy, feeble virtue that can't stand to be mingled with poverty or grief or uncertainty or trouble. No. On the contrary. Peace, the shalom of God, *is* peace *because* it dares to dip its head and seek us out in the caves and the closets and the dark recesses of our minds where we tremble and doubt and shiver with pain.

We hide in search of peace, and yet the strange and oddly discomfiting quality of peace is this: it is the peace of God that *seeks us out*, and when it finds us, we are often in the lowest places. It is beyond our comprehension. It passes right by our understanding. And when it wraps its tender arms around us, peace lures us out of hiding by seeing right through us to who we really have been all along.

"God is with you, O Mighty Warrior," we hear a voice calling to us from the mouth of the cave where we have hidden ourselves (see Judg. 6:12). We have made makeshift

146

accommodations, and we have usurped our resources and co-opted them to be used in tasks for which they were never intended. We have used winepresses to thresh out the grain from the chaff. We are poor in spirit, and inside the cavities of our chests, our hearts mourn deep within us. We shrink into our smallness on the dark side of the cave, and we label ourselves with words of insignificance and incompetence and impotence and ignorance.

When we hear that voice saying, "God is with you, O Mighty Warrior," we think we must be dreaming. Or we convince ourselves the caller has come calling on someone other than us.

Forty years after Sisera lay bleeding and dead on the floor of Jael's tent, the people of God "went back to doing evil in God's sight." And so "GOD put them under the domination of Midian for seven years" (Judg. 6:1).

The Midianites were merciless. They plundered the people of Israel. The Midianites invaded and camped in the fields of the Israelites. The Midianites took possession of the Israelites' livestock. When harvest time came, the Midianites beat the people of God to the punch and gathered up all the food, leaving God's people with nothing to eat. And in Judges 6 we are told, "The People of Israel, reduced to grinding poverty by Midian, cried out to God for help" (v. 6).

Grinding poverty. Those two words hold a world of weight between them. Those who know or have known poverty can attest to the way poverty might rob a soul of peace. But poverty that grinds away at a soul can strip it of its hope as well and send a soul that feels small and insignificant into hiding.

What happens when you've lost the ability or the desire to dream? What if you have no idea what your calling or your purpose might be? When it feels like all the cards of life are stacked against you, your dreams have been reduced to dust, and God has decided to keep his thoughts from you? What then?

Christians are not immune to these feelings of insignificance. We find ourselves depleted and we languish in poverty of spirit or soul when we muddy the waters of our relationship with Christ by choosing to measure and compare the impact of our spiritual influence in our small corner of this world with the spiritual influence of others in their corners of the world. We are doomed before we fire up our calculator, refresh our browser, or unhinge our tape measure from our tool belt, because no matter where we look, we will always find someone who seems to be better equipped with and wielding greater spiritual influence than we are. But God is not counting. He is not measuring. God is not keeping score.

So what about those of us who have forgotten how to dream? What about the ones whose dreams seem indefinitely deferred, or who don't even know why they're here in the first place? In the scheme of things, and taken on its own, your dream may not even show up on your radar screen. But we might be looking in all the wrong places.

When I meet people who ask me, "What about me? I don't even know how to dream. I don't know where to begin," I hear in their question the start of a dream. If this sounds familiar to you, if you have been wondering why you can't seem to latch on to your purpose, let me just say I hold you in high esteem.

When the world or time or circumstance or even tragedy has beaten us down and we fight to find our voice again, it is no small thing to notice the desire in a heart for dreams that have gone missing. What if you didn't even notice the vacancy? What if you were beyond the point of believing there might be a dream or a purpose or a plan for you?

148

Doesn't it mean something to notice the empty seat where a dream should be?

I believe it does. Noticing the absence of a dream is actually the beginning of a dream. It is the seed of hope, planted deep in the heart; it is deep calling to deep. At first it feels pointless and lacking in meaning. It seems too small to be given any credit. It doesn't feel sturdy enough for us to shift any weight over onto it. Losing sight of a dream, or feeling as if we wander through this life without purpose, seems so very opposite of all the grand and big things our world likes to celebrate, doesn't it?

God sees things differently. With God, the small things matter for bigness too. Maybe you feel as though you must have been absent when God was handing out purpose, but if that's what you've been thinking, I'm here to tell you you've been duped. You may look at your life and see a dead end, or a dreamless heart, or a person with no purpose. You might think big is all that matters, but there's a new song to sing, sweet thing. There are so many stories in the Bible that bear this out. Three of these stories come to my mind right away.

In the Old Testament, with a famine raging and the water in the brook dried up, the prophet Elijah asked a widow for a glass of water and, as she started out to fetch the water, also for a piece of bread. But she didn't have any bread. All she had was "a handful of flour in a jar and a little olive oil in a jug" (1 Kings 17:12 NIV). It wasn't much at all. The widow had plans to fry up that flour in the olive oil as a last meal for her and her son. They would eat the fried flour and then they would die, because they had nothing left. But Elijah said to her:

Don't be afraid. Go home and do as you have said. But first make *a small loaf of bread* for me from what you have and bring it to me, and then make something for yourself and your son. For this is what the LORD, the God of Israel, says: "The jar of flour will not be used up and the jug of oil will not run dry until the day the LORD sends rain on the land." (1 Kings 17:13–14 NIV, emphasis added)

The widow did it. She cooked the flour with the oil, and after that, she and her son and Elijah the prophet were always supplied with food. The containers of flour and oil were never empty.

All that was required was the making of a small loaf of bread. No large buffet was requested. No fatted calf was expected. There was no mention of courses or multiple servings. Simply a small loaf of bread, which was made by scraping the bottom of the barrel for the last little bits of flour.

God hears our desire for purpose; he knows when our dreams have turned to dust and all we know to do is figure out how to eat that last meal before giving it all up for good. "Make the bread," he says to us when we find ourselves scraping the bottom of the barrel and coming up with nothing. Do the next thing. Do the next, small thing. God is not measuring by the world's standards. God set the world in motion, and God is making all things new—every little thing.

In the very first verses of Luke 21, Jesus watches as people present their offerings in the worship service. He watches the rich people as they place money in the collection plate, and then a widow drops two pennies into the plate and Jesus says, "The plain truth is that this widow has given by far the largest offering today. All these others made offerings that they'll never miss; she gave extravagantly what she couldn't afford—she gave her all!" (vv. 3–4).

Jesus sees two pennies—something you and I might step over if we saw them lying in the middle of the road as we walk around the neighborhood for exercise. Heck, we may even vacuum right over two pennies should they find their way to our living room floors—and Jesus calls them the largest offering of the day. Extravagant! Surely, on the church accountant's balance sheet, the offerings the rich people dropped into the plate measured up as "bigger and better." But that's not the way Jesus saw it.

Two pennies may look small to some, but for this woman, those two pennies were something she really couldn't afford to give up. When she went home, she would notice those two pennies were gone. Those two pennies were all she had and their absence would be noticed, in the same way people notice when a dream has stopped beating in their heart. The dream slips away and we wonder if anyone else noticed.

Jesus takes note of these things. He knows what a big deal it is when all that's left seems like not enough. It is an extravagant thing to take your beaten down and dreamless heart, stagger your way up to Jesus, and whisper to him, "Hey, what about me?"

In Matthew 25, Jesus reminds us that God notices our smallest actions. No small thing escapes him. Jesus paints a scene for his disciples of God welcoming some into his kingdom. He says:

Come, you who are blessed by my Father; take your inheritance, the kingdom prepared for you since the creation of the world. For I was hungry and you gave me something to eat, I was thirsty and you gave me something to drink, I was a stranger and you invited me in, I needed clothes and you clothed me, I was sick and you looked after me, I was in prison and you came to visit me. (vv. 34–36 NIV)

But those being invited into the kingdom don't even realize they've done anything that matters. I am always struck by their confusion. Had they been going through life reaching for big dreams or trying to make a big splash in the world to catch God's attention, their efforts probably would have fallen short of the small things they did that actually brought God great delight as they went about the business of living their ordinary days. Those being welcomed into the kingdom (they are called "the righteous") are incredulous in their response to God. They wrinkle their brows and raise their eyes upward, as if searching inside their brains for a memory. They say:

Lord, when did we see you hungry and feed you, or thirsty and give you something to drink? When did we see you a stranger and invite you in, or needing clothes and clothe you? When did we see you sick or in prison and go to visit you? (vv. 37–39 NIV)

In verse 40, God, the King, replies to them, "Truly I tell you, whatever you did for one of the least of these brothers and sisters of mine, you did for me" (NIV).

I think I might be inclined to say, "But it was only a glass of water!" But that wouldn't be fair now, would it? God, the King, does not discount even the glass of water given (perhaps even absentmindedly) from the heart, instead of as a project.

Perhaps it would do the world a bit of good if we decided to reconsider the things we label small.

We are not alone in our misconceptions about what the world considers small. In their book *Workplace Grace*, Bill Peel and Walt Larimore remind us to consider the truth about our methods of measurement:

> Unfortunately, many Christians think spiritual influence is about "big things." This should not surprise us because Jesus's disciples were often fixated on big things.
>
> James and John wanted to call down fire from heaven to put nonbelievers in their place. Peter wanted to walk on water. And knowing which disciples ranked the highest and had the most authority was a big deal. Throughout the gospels, we see Jesus trying to teach his disciples that spiritual influence is not about doing big things. It is about being a servant.
>
> When it comes to carrying out his plans, it seems God has a penchant for small things that we may deem insignificant. Moses's wooden staff was nothing special, but God used it to confront the heart of the most powerful ruler of the ancient world. David used a small stone to kill a giant. With one word Jesus could have produced a catered meal for thousands, but instead he chose to use a small boy's lunch.
>
> God has not changed. He wants to use everyday things we may consider small . . . to accomplish big things for his kingdom.[1]

God called Gideon out from his hiding place and whittled down Gideon's army from tens of thousands to just three hundred men. And God used that small army to defeat the

153

Midianites, redeem the people of God from their soul-crushing poverty, and restore them to peace and hopefulness once again.

We know Gideon wasn't convinced of God's game plan. We've seen how Gideon doubted, and he even tested God by asking for a sign that God really intended to use Gideon to pull off this upset against the Midianites. That may be the part of Gideon's story with which we can most relate. We look at our circumstances and our sphere of influence and we stand there, convinced God has come calling at the mouth of the wrong cave. But if Gideon teaches us anything, it's that doubt is no match for God's intentions.

God doesn't need us to spread the good news of his love throughout the earth. But God created us, from the very beginning, to be co-creators along with him. He wants us to participate in his plan of redemption and restoration. He was the first to put his hand to the plow, and he invites us to join him in kingdom-building work. Hard to believe, right? God invites us along in the greatest adventure of all time. He calls to us and clears a space for us at the workbench of new life, the same way we call our children to join us in a seat beside us in the combine at harvest time, or to help sift the flour for a loved one's birthday cake, or to sit beside us on a piano bench and learn to locate middle C in a sea of eighty-eight ivory keys.

Can I encourage you to downsize your thinking just a bit? Sometimes thinking in terms of changing the world, or even thinking of what many call kingdom-building work, is just way too much to try to comprehend. What if we each took stock of the place where our feet are planted and considered the possibility that those feet of yours belong to a mighty warrior, and that mighty warrior is you?

Don't pay attention to the doubts in your heart or the weaknesses you know about yourself. Don't entertain the notion that God couldn't use someone like you. Let go of your grip on fear. Just look at your feet. Go ahead. Take a deep breath and look at them, and then consider where they're planted. How many steps would you have to take to make a difference for good? For God? Probably not as many as you once thought. After all, didn't Jael put an end to Sisera's reign of terror, right there on the dirt floor of her very own tent?

Mighty warrior, indeed.

Jael's one act of courage changed the course of history for the people of God. Her actions were brave, and she was filled with courage. Or fear. Or hopelessness. We really can't be sure, can we? The Bible doesn't bother itself with details in stories like these. All we can do is try to put ourselves in Jael's shoes and imagine what we'd be feeling if we were in her place. We read the stories of Gideon and Jael and Moses and Rahab and all the rest, and we are tempted to imagine they must have had something we don't have and never will. If that's the path we let our minds take, we have wandered down the wrong path, that's for sure. We have *exactly* what they had. *You* have exactly what they had.

The God of these stories is the exact same God who extends an invitation to you today to climb up next to him on the piano bench and play your one note in the symphony he's writing on the manuscript in front of him. God is not measuring your one note against anyone else's. He doesn't value *big* over *willing*. He doesn't require you to "measure up" before he extends the invitation. He doesn't think Jael or Gideon or all the rest had better or more significant assignments than the one note you are meant to play right where your feet are planted.

Driving a stake through the head of a dictatorial tyrant takes courage, yes. But it also takes courage to live a life of faith in the boardroom when everyone else is voting yes on a strategy that causes you to question the moral and ethical foundations and repercussions of that strategy. It takes courage to invite the new person in the neighborhood to join your family for dinner. It takes courage to have the hard conversations with your teenager about character and choices and consequences. It takes courage to admit to your spouse that you've been letting your eyes or your heart or your body wander into unfaithfulness. It takes courage to apologize to a friend you've offended and to confess that you were wrong. It takes courage to admit your need for help and your inability to conquer an addiction or an eating disorder or a destructive behavioral pattern by the sheer force of your will. Sometimes it takes courage simply to get dinner on the table or to show up for your children at the first light of the new day. Sometimes the smallest steps we take are actually the biggest.

You have exactly what it takes, mighty warrior.

The Hebrew word for courage suggests the idea of being "strong in the feet" or "swift footed."[2] In other words, more than having a resolute mind or a heart of steel, courage is the willingness to take a step in the direction of God's invitation toward us. "Stand firm then, with the belt of truth buckled around your waist, with the breastplate of righteousness in place, and with your feet fitted with the readiness that comes from the gospel of peace" (Eph. 6:14–15 NIV).

Remember, it is always about God. All of the steps we take are always about loving God and loving people. No matter what. This is not a competition. The smallest gifts matter to God.

My mom wrote a song about a child who gives a dandelion to her mother. Ask any grown-up, and most of them will tell you a dandelion is a weed. We slide our dollar bills across the counter at the local hardware store each spring, and in exchange we get a bag or a bottle of chemicals, expertly crafted to eliminate the bright yellow polka dots from our front yards. We've determined the dandelion brings down the value of our home and disrupts our hard-earned curb appeal.

But my mother knew differently. She'd received the offering of a bouquet of dandelions, sprouting from the dimpled fist of a child whose heart knew only that it was compelled to give a gift of gratitude. Here are the words to the chorus of that song my mom wrote:

> I never knew a dandelion was a weed.
> I never thought about its seed.
> I picked them only to
> Give to my mother,
> They said, "I love you,
> There is no other quite like you."[3]

Perhaps you've been the recipient of a gift like this yourself. Perhaps you've received a necklace made of macaroni noodles, or a finger-painted work of art, or the gift of muddied hands pressed against your cheeks to draw you close and kiss you gently on your chin. You did not scoff at the gift giver, did you? You did not relegate the gift to the trash bin or the compost pile. You received the gift in the spirit it was given, with love and grace and sincerity of heart.

Your one step in the direction of God's invitation may seem small and insignificant to you. You may feel you have nothing to offer God, or that your offering is a nuisance to be eliminated, or that your offering actually diminishes the kingdom and this world. You could not be further from the truth. Your step in the direction of God's invitation sends the same message to God that the dandelion sends the mother in the song my mom wrote: "I love you, God. There is no other quite like you."

Don't measure your step. Just take the step.

If you were to dare to dream again, what would be the first step you might take? What two pennies would you offer? What small loaf of bread might you bake? What cup of water would you pour?

All around us, in cotton socks with the heel worn thin, walk mighty warriors whose stories will never qualify them for the cover of a magazine, or a seat on the stage next to Oprah, or a book deal, or a recording contract, or even an honorable mention. But their small acts of courage (or fear or hopelessness) are making a world of difference in their communities, in their families, in their churches, at their dinner tables, in their marriages. They move an inch in the direction of God's invitation, not knowing what comes next or where the path will lead, and God infuses his Holy Spirit into their skills and talents and passions and their smallest grain of willingness to follow where Christ leads, and he shapes them into the everlasting work of redemption and restoration. Who says miracles don't happen anymore?

We can take solace and find comfort in the biblical accounts of people doing seemingly insignificant things that mattered for eternity. But sometimes those stories seem so far removed from the everyday lives we're living, with our deadlines and our laundry and our grass that needs mowing and the recycling bin that keeps overflowing. We need to be convinced these types of miracles are still happening today. And they are! It's just that we're right in the middle of these everyday moments. We are living them out, not knowing the impact they're making on the world. Surely the woman who baked that small loaf of bread and the woman who gave her last two pennies had no idea we'd still be talking about them and learning from them and being encouraged by them right up to this very day.

The Bible goes to great lengths to show us that all the people on its pages were ordinary and average, doing one little thing after another, rooted in trust, grounded in good news, and drenched in fear or hopelessness. We take the good with the bad, and God is gracious to give us both, as a reminder that every good and perfect thing starts with God (see James 1:17). Even people like Moses and Noah and Abraham and Sarah had their weaknesses and made their missteps. When Paul talks about the prophet Elijah, and how Elijah prayed to God for it to rain and God heard Elijah's prayer, Paul points out for all to see, "Elijah was a human being, even as we are." (James 5:17 NIV). The only one who rose above it all was Jesus. As for the rest of the people in all the stories in the Bible, God filled them up with his Holy Spirit and breathed life into their dreams and their plans, and God, through ordinary people who did ordinary things, made miracles happen that changed the world for good.

Is it only a miracle when Jesus spits in the dirt and then smears mud on a blind man's eyes and restores the blind man's sight? Why can't it also be a miracle when you press through the doubt and fear and step from the dark recesses of the cave and into the light of God's invitation to you? Why can't it also be a miracle when we put away our tape measures and our calculators and stop comparing our purpose with someone else's purpose? Why can't it also be a miracle to stand up on our two feet and celebrate the gift of every little thing God calls us to? Even if no one notices but him? Wouldn't that be a miracle too? Wouldn't it be worship? Wouldn't it count?

Yes. It would count. It does count. It matters. It is miraculous.

★☆✗★★✗ **9** ✗☆★★✗★

We Are the Lucky Ones

> In the beginning God created the heavens and the earth.
> Now the earth was formless and empty, darkness was
> over the surface of the deep, and the Spirit of God was
> hovering over the waters. And God said, "Let there be
> light," and there was light.
>
> Genesis 1:1–3 NIV

Gideon was one of the lucky ones. So were Mary, and Noah, and Abraham, and Moses, and all of the disciples. In fact, on the surface, it would seem most of the people in the Bible got a better deal from God than you might believe you're getting. After all, every single one of them seemed to get a clear, indisputable message from God with marching orders that practically included a GPS system in the back pocket.

There was no reading between the lines to determine what it was God wanted them to do. There was no fuzziness in the directive he issued to them.

God to Mary: You are going to be the mother of the Messiah. Name him Jesus. (Luke 1:31)

God to Noah: I need you to build an ark and build it to these unique specifications, which I will outline for you in great detail. (Gen. 6:11–21)

God to Abraham: Get your whole family together and move. I'll show you the way. (Gen. 12:1)

God to Abraham again: You and Sarah are going to have a son! (Gen. 18:10)

God to Abraham yet again (God gave Abraham lots of instructions): Take your son Isaac and sacrifice him on the mountain. (Gen. 22:2) (Not so appealing but still very clear.)

God to Moses: Go to Egypt and tell Pharaoh to let my people go. (Exod. 3)

God to Gideon: Mighty warrior! Go in the strength you have and save Israel from the hand of Midian. (Judg. 6:12–16)

Jesus to the disciples: Follow me. (Matt. 4:19)

God to me: Silence. Not even crickets. (Personal experience.)

Isn't that the way it feels? Maybe you've been asking the same questions others ask when trying to figure out which small step to take that will somehow make a difference in the world for good or for God: Why is it that God was so clear back in the Bible days and today he seems to be talking to everyone but me? And if I do have an idea about what it is I'm supposed to do in the world for good or for God, how do I know that's not my voice in my head instead of God's voice in my heart? How come I can't hear anything? What am I doing wrong? And when I do try to do what I think God is telling me to do, why does it always seem to fall flat? Why do so many other people seem to have this figured out and I just keep feeling like I'm spinning my wheels?

You rise early in the morning, and while you may not be out selecting wool and flax like that woman we've all grown to know (see Prov. 31:13), you are doing your best to spend a little quiet time with God. Or maybe you're not a morning person (join the club!) and you find yourself more likely to be the last one to lay your body in bed at night, quietly turning the pages in your Bible or shaping ink into prayers on the pages of your journal while everyone else in your family is sound asleep. Maybe you simply go through the day, saying prayers that sound like this: "Help!" "Oops!" "Good grief!"

Let's agree right here and now not to get caught up in form. I mean, there are as many ways to spend time with God as there are people on this earth. There is no right or wrong way to spend time with God. For some of us, having a specific time of day set aside to study and pray and to meditate and to sing, and perhaps even to dance, is the best and most direct route to communion with God. But it's not the only way.

We do a grave disservice to a number of people when we insist on making everyone fit their relationship with God into a form that doesn't match (and in some cases actually betrays) their personality. For some of us, setting an appointment with God feels like an act of rebellion. It doesn't mean we don't want to spend time with God. But what if the formulas and neat outlines others point to as "the way" to connect with God often spell out, in neatly printed letters, the first step in a downward spiral for those who thrive with less structure and planning?

Our relationships with God are as unique and as individual as the people we are. There will never be another you, and God meant it that way. He is the ultimate Creator, with more unique combinations of DNA at his disposal than there are grains of sand on all the beaches in the whole world. He did not create you and place you on this earth and then look at what he'd done, twist his lips, press his eyebrows together in disappointment, and say, "Oops! That is not what I had in mind." And might I prevail upon you here not to get caught up in the theology of whether or not God actually placed you on the earth however many years ago? Please don't miss the point here.

Whether your particular theology leads you to lean toward new earth or old earth, nature or nurture, homeschool or public school, breast or bottle, big government or smaller government, war or peace, creation or evolution, or whatever and all points in between, the bottom line is this: God loves you, exactly the way you are, period.

That's simply the way it is.

God's love for you is not dependent upon what you believe about him or about the world and how it came to be or how it will end or if it will end. It does not matter what you think about who should love whom and who gets to decide what about this thing or the other. All of that is worth trying to figure out between you and God if that's what floats your boat, but no matter what you decide about it all, it can't change the fact that no matter what you believe or think or do or say; no matter how you vote or if you vote; no matter if you have been married twenty times or never; no matter if you go to church every single Sunday and Wednesday or if you've given up on church and the Church and God and the whole shebang, you cannot do a single solitary thing about the fact that God loves you, exactly the way you are. You don't have to believe it, but that doesn't make it any less true.

Wait. Let's back up, because this may be the most important thing there ever was.

God loves you, exactly the way you are. Please don't miss that. Buried here, in these pages and chapters and paragraphs and sentences and letters, is the most important thing: God's love for you cannot be reversed or changed or denied or fumbled or faked. His love for you is real, and it is forever.

This is not a competition. No matter what the magazine on your coffee table tells you, this is not a competition.

I am typing this out in the sunroom of my house where my desk sits surrounded on three sides by windows, and through the speaker over my right shoulder, Roberta Flack's rich, mahogany drenched voice is crooning the words to "The First Time Ever I Saw Your Face." This is no accident, because, say what you will, God can speak to us through songs sung by Roberta Flack because God is the God of creation and music is art, and we can be co-creators with God when we plant flowers, or paint walls, or design code, or cut hair, or sew curtains, or sweep our dirt floors, or pour a foundation, or dig a well, or cook a meal, or sing a song. And what I want to do, with Roberta Flack singing here in the background, is to sit across from you wherever you are right now and unwrap this song for you as a love song. I would simply be the delivery person. The message comes from God to you:

from the moment God first laid eyes on you, he was head over heels in love.

God loves you, exactly the way you are, period.

You have a right to be here. You were created on purpose. Regardless of what anyone else may have to say about it, you being here is a good thing. A very good thing.

In the account of creation, as chronicled in the opening paragraphs of the Bible, God created everything you could possibly imagine, plus some things you might never imagine on your own (Have you ever seen a leafy seadragon?), and when he looked at everything he had made, God saw that it was good. But it was after God created people that he looked around at his creation and declared that it was very good (see Gen. 1:31).

God looks at you and God is very pleased. You don't have to do a single thing—not one thing—to make it so.

My husband introduced me to *Star Trek* in the early stages of our relationship. He is a devoted fan of the show, and it doesn't matter if we're watching the William Shatner/Leonard Nimoy version or the *Next Generation* version with Patrick Stewart and LeVar Burton. *Star Trek* is one of my husband's favorites.

When we first got married, we moved from Michigan to New York State, where my husband was a seminary student. It was a good life, and we had a great time as newlyweds. We were living in married housing in a Tudor-style apartment building with single-paned windows that opened with a turn-crank and that frosted over in the winter. Each night, the heat to our building was turned off at the main outlet by someone whom we knew only as "Maintenance," and in the morning the radiator clanged and hissed and sputtered to life after the heat was turned back on, just before dawn. But we barely noticed the cold.

We were starry-eyed with our new life and love, and we grinned incessantly. We tested the floor beneath our newly married status and found it solid and spreading out in every direction with new opportunities and bold strokes of independence. We married young. He was twenty-four and I was twenty-two. These days, when we pull out our album of wedding photos, we look at ourselves in those images and shake our heads. "What were you thinking?" we ask those two young faces staring back at us. Of course, we wouldn't change a thing.

Except, back in that tiny apartment in the Tudor-style apartment building, our tiny, portable RCA television didn't offer any episodes of *Star Trek*. "The only thing missing," my new husband would say to me as we maneuvered around each other in our miniature kitchen with its itty-bitty apartment stove, "is *Star Trek*." If he could have changed anything about our new life together behind the freezing cold windows, my new husband would have wished for *Star Trek*.

For months we soldiered on without the voyagers of the starship *Enterprise* and their continuing mission. We violated the "no pets" rule set down for us by "Maintenance" and brought home a rescue dog, and we cooked Thanksgiving dinner. We counted our pennies, right up until the last minute, and bought the fattest Christmas tree I've ever seen—one of just a handful still left on the lot. We decorated that tree entirely in red lights (because those were only the lights left on the shelf at the discount store at the very last minute) and from the street, our seminary apartment looked like a Christmas bordello. We confiscated plastic molded trays from the refectory and used them as sleds on the snow-covered slope

167

beneath an ebony-clouded winter night sky while the seminary sat perched above us—the proverbial beacon on the hill. We drove through the park in the spring with the melodious scent of lilac bushes in the air, and we windsurfed until the sun washed the surface of the lake like watercolors from an artist's tin. We understood the word *bliss*, and we melded into one. And then one day we turned on the television, and there it was: *Star Trek: The Next Generation*. It was official. Our lives had reached perfection.

In *Star Trek: The Next Generation*, Captain Picard issues directives to his first officer, Will Riker. Captain Picard calls his first officer "Number One," and when he makes a request, Captain Picard says, "Make it so, Number One." And Number One makes it so.

Sitting on our small couch in our pint-sized apartment, watching our scaled-down television, Harry and I would look at each other and say, "Make it so."

With God, because of his great love for us, it is already made so. Everything. When Jesus said from the cross, "It is finished" (John 19:30 NIV), it really was.

It really is.

When it comes to God's love for you, there is nothing you need to do to make it so. You don't need to do good deeds or save the world (or even your own family) or be the perfect parent or Sunday school teacher or accountant or community volunteer or Bible reader or writer in order for God to take great delight in you. God loves you because he is love and he is unable to do anything but love you.

You don't need to have a certain type of quiet time or memorize a certain number of Bible verses. None of that will make God love you more. Each one of these beautiful and sacred

168

disciplines, sacraments, habits, and rituals—prayer, worship, Bible reading, confession, communion, Sabbath, and more— is created for us, not the other way around. Just as with the Sabbath, they were created for us as a way to help focus our attention on God when our thoughts or our hands or our time or our talents or our hopes get away from us on our continuing mission to know God and enjoy him forever, and to love God and to love people well.

God is for you.

God is close to you and he is behind you and before you and beside you. God is in you. This is not the same thing as saying we are each little gods. Our lives are sacred and holy, but we are not gods and goddesses or even angels. In the book of Psalms, David reminds us we were created just a little lower than the angels (see 8:5), and still, God is head over heels in love with us.

Only God is God.

What you are is loved by God, exactly as you are, and when you let that be the truth (which is not the same as understanding what it means to be loved in such a way by such a God), you begin to feel as if you might just be able to catch your breath and discard the soiled sheets you've wrapped around yourself. You begin to throw away the empty lies about yourself, and you take heart and find courage to let fear be fear while you step across the threshold into the adventure God has been keeping just for you.

There will never be another you. God means for it to be that way. There will never be another combination of DNA on this earth that looks the same as yours. And so there will never be another impact made like the one you will make with your stunningly magnificent life.

169

Do not miss the importance of the impact your life can make. Don't miscalculate and come to the conclusion that your contributions don't matter because they haven't made the cover of *Time* magazine. God isn't measuring things the way the world measures them. God is not impressed with the spotlights we so ravenously crave. If you're searching for the spotlight and you find yourself in one, you have what you've been looking for. Nothing more. Nothing less. But ask anyone who has spent any time in the spotlight, and they will tell you the spotlight fades and eventually someone you may never see—someone whose name you may only know as "Maintenance"—will turn the spotlight off or direct its glow on someone else who will occupy its small circle for a few short moments of recognition.

If a personal spotlight is what you're looking for, you've set your sights in the wrong direction. Hang on. I am not saying spotlights are wrong. They are not. But if it's your goal to be in the spotlight and you find yourself there and wonder why it feels so empty, there is a reason for that.

You are a light set on a hill to help point people to God.

Right from the very opening words of the Gospel of John, we are reminded that Jesus is the Word of God, present with God from before the beginning of time. God created everything by this Word when, in the Genesis account, God spoke into nothingness and said, "Let there be," and there was (see 1:3 NIV). In Latin the phrase is *ex nihilo*, which means "out of nothing." There was nothing here, and when God, his Holy Spirit hovering over the face of the deep, spoke into the nothingness, the world began. The first chapter of the Gospel of John goes on to explain to us that life itself is in Jesus Christ. It is because God said—the Word—that everything was. Everything is. So lift up your head and take a look around you. Everything around you that lives and breathes and grows and has its being—all of it gets its life from the life that is in and comes to us through Jesus, who is the very Word of God who spoke this world into existence.

Breathe in.

Breathe out.

How do you break this down so that it is anything but a glistening testament of glory? The gift of life is ours because of (in, by, with, among, at, through) Jesus Christ, whether we believe he is who he says he is or not. And as John goes on to tell us, it is that life—the life in Christ—that is the light of the world. The light shines in the darkness, and darkness cannot overcome it (see John 1:1–5).

Now, let's enter slowly here and perhaps take off our shoes, because this great God is holy and it would be a dangerous thing to believe that because of the life of Christ in us, we are somehow equal to God. We are not. Only God is God. And let's remember what that means for us. What we are is this: we are loved by God and lit up from the inside because of God. We have the light of life in us, and when we give control of our lives over to him, the Holy Spirit fills us with power, and we become witnesses to the light of Christ, pointing the light of our life to him so that his glory is on display.

Seeking the spotlight for ourselves is empty and shallow. It sounds like clanging gongs and tinkling cymbals, and it is good for a moment, but then it fades into hollow darkness and clings to the bottom of our shoes despite our attempts to scrape it off, because we were made for so much more than the spotlight.

171

The Gospel of John spells out our relationship to God in one sentence when introducing us to John the Baptist, the cousin of Christ: "He [John the Baptist] was not that Light, but was sent to bear witness of that Light" (John 1:8 KJV). John the Baptist, just like you and me, was sent to bear witness to the light of life that is in Christ Jesus. Jesus is, indeed, the Light of the World, and we are here to testify to that. We are here to agree with God that the gift of life is in Jesus, and that life is the Light of the World.

Do you see that? Is it possible those words caused a small shift in your heart? You are here to be loved by God and to love God. You are here to direct the light of your life to Jesus so that his glory is on display.

When we read the stories in the Bible of Mary and Moses and Abraham and Gideon and Rahab and the disciples and all the rest, it is so easy to believe they moved through their days thinking, "This is it! I am doing a great thing for God!" It's easy to believe they were clear and confident in the mission they carried out. It's easy to think they had counted the cost and they were pleased with where their investment would land them. We have sealed the flannel board images of these Bible characters in our minds, and we are sure of their happy endings.

We know Moses got the people of God to the Promised Land, but we forget he was a murderer whose temper kept him from getting there with them. We remember God's promise that Abraham would be the father of many nations, but we forget Ishmael and the enmity between him and his half brother throughout the generations. We sing songs about Noah and his ark and how he loaded it up, two by two, and how he and his family landed safely on dry ground. But we forget his drunkenness and how that left him vulnerable to his desperate daughters. David slept with Uriah's wife and then had Uriah killed. Rahab was a prostitute. Gideon was a coward.

In the pages of our Bibles, we read about Jesus calling the Twelve to come and follow him. We read the Gospels and we forget these men were hell-raisers and castoffs, living on the fringes of their communities and never considered by anyone to be biblical scholars with solid theologies. And while Judas may have been the one who told the authorities where they could find Jesus, every single one of the disciples turned on Jesus in the moments when one might argue he needed them the most.

In other words, all of these people—from Genesis to Revelation—were human. Just like you. Just like me.

You've probably heard the saying that comparison is the thief of joy, but not if you're comparing yourself to this cast of characters.

They were no different from you. They were living ordinary, everyday lives. To varying degrees, they were trying to stay out of trouble, work in their chosen professions, and provide for their families. Some of the heroes of the faith that we read about in the Bible were clearly focused on trying to please God in the days before we meet them, and others began their journey far from God. It didn't matter. God invited them anyway. There were no prerequisites, no entrance exams, and no vetting processes.

You are God's perfect candidate for this adventure. Your busted-up, messed over, boring, uneventful, bruised and battered, disappointed, twisted, ho-hum, average, everyday life is exactly what God is looking for. The writer of 2 Corinthians reminds us we are earthen vessels into which God

173

pours his Spirit and through which he works out his purposes (see 4:7 KJV). If we were anything more than humble, earthen vessels, we might forget that the excellency of the power (the KJV is so good at spelling out the full majesty) is God's and not ours.

Are you still looking at your life, turning it over in your hands and declaring to the vast expanse of hopelessness, "I have nothing to offer"? Have you forgotten, mighty warrior, that God does his very best work from nothing? Ex nihilo.

In the beginning, when the earth was formless and shapeless and chaotic, God's Holy Spirit hovered over the vast expanse and stepped into that void of nothingness, and God, through the Word that is the Christ, said, "Let there be . . ." And there was. There is.

The difference between us and the vacuous wilderness of the world before God stepped in and spoke order into it—the great difference between that and us—is will.

At creation, God spoke and there was, not only because God is God but also because all of everything was surrendered to God. There was no resistance. The vast expanse of chaos didn't have a committee meeting or a list of pros and cons for deciding whether to participate in what it was God was calling forth. There was no one and nothing with which to compare, and there was absolutely no concept of having anything to lose. No ego. No mortgage. No 401(k). No reputation. No career. No five-star reviews. No Midianites. No thoughts of yellow life preservers or multicolored parachutes. No arms outstretched across the passenger seat. No sheets to hide behind. No bandits waiting around the bend.

God created everything, and then God created us in God's image and blew into us the breath of life—the *imago dei*. And

174

there we were, exercising our will: thinking for ourselves and being logical and making our own decisions and choosing what to believe and deciding whom to follow and assigning value and becoming attached to things and to people. There is not a glitch in the system. This is the way God planned it because God, who all at once is Father, Son, and Holy Spirit, values relationship, and as anyone who's ever been in a relationship knows, no one wants a relationship built on obligation or compulsion. And so God created us with the ability to choose our own way, knowing we might not choose him.

We get to choose. We get to decide whether to let God's "Make it so" and "Let there be" bear fruit in our lives. From the beginning of time, we have been deciding whether to surrender our agendas and desires and hopes and dreams to God's agenda and desire and hopes and dreams for us. We've been trying to get beyond the great liar's trap, so expertly set for Adam and Eve and into which they fell. Rather than agreeing with God that God is God and God's plan for them was good, Adam and Eve got distracted and believed the idea that they could be like God.

We've been trying to see the truth of God through the legacy of Adam and Eve's miscalculation. Yet God calls to us from the other side of their error and reminds us of his original plan for us: to know him, to love him, and—through the work of our hands and from one generation to the next—to spread the image of God, the *imago dei*, through the earth, clearing space for redemption and restoration.

Adam and Eve said no to God's invitation. They thought they could create a better offer for themselves, and so they cashed in their relationship with God for a taste of the forbidden fruit, and then they found themselves desperately trying to hide their sin behind a few fig leaves.

The only difference between humanity and the rest of God's creation is our will. We get to choose. Will we choose God's way or our own way?

The heroes of the Bible agreed with God. They were not pure in heart or sinless or superhuman or extraordinarily brave of their own accord. Have you been comparing your life to some contemporary sojourner who seems to have it all together? Have you measured your life and your accomplishments and the size of your dreams against theirs and found yours wanting? Have you begun to categorize the works of God as great and small and found the work of God in you just doesn't measure up?

God's instructions to you today couldn't be more clear. He has written his plans for you among the stars and in the grains of sand on the beach, and he has breathed his dream for you into your DNA and pressed his palm against your heart. What God is calling out of you is you. Your hopes and dreams. Your personality. Your fears and your miscalculations. God has knit you together by his spoken Word, and he has made available to you the presence of the Holy Spirit. God looks at you and what he sees is always good.

You, and only you, can express a particular and specific aspect of God's character in this world of ours, and (in case you didn't hear it the first time) what God is calling out of you is you. The difference between you and the rest of God's created world is your ability to turn to God when he calls to you from the mouth of the cave and say yes. Or no. We are the ones who exercise our will, and God, in his great love for us, allows us the freedom to do just that.

Check the record for yourself.

Mary's Magnificat, Noah's first step into the forest to gather wood that would become an ark, Abraham's knife raised over the chest of his promised son, Moses's meeting with Pharaoh, Gideon's march against the Midianites with three hundred men, each one of the disciples who left everything they had to follow Jesus, and all the rest.

It's not always a fast and easy yes. We know that Abraham laughed at the promise of God, and Moses tried to get someone else to convince Pharaoh he should let God's people go. Gideon asked for proof several times, and the disciples weren't even all in on the night Jesus was betrayed. But they said yes. Bit by bit, along the journey, they each said yes. And God worked through them. Right where they stood, and just as they were.

You will only ever get this life. If you're like me, you want this one life to count for something. You want it to be more than a chasing after the wind. You want to know your feet on the earth beneath you meant something and that you lived a life of significance. But what does that mean? How will we know? When the last day comes for us, how will we know we counted for more than ashes and dust?

Here's the thing about that: we will know. When we take our last breath and cross from this side of the veil to the other, we will know. We will be confident on that day because we will know even as we are known. There can't be words to describe how it will feel to know just how significant our life on this earth has been and how much we matter to God. Until then, we can strive our way to the top of all the lists and the seats at the best parties and the recognition and accolades and awards that lose their value. We can measure ourselves against one another and castigate ourselves in front of mirrors

177

and through the watches of the night. Or we can agree with God that he loves us, just the way we are. Because of God's great love for us, we are not consumed (see Lam. 3:22). We already measure up. We have what it takes.

You matter. From the first breath you took when you entered this world, you mattered. From the instant your life began, God has loved you.

Would it be all right with you if God took over from here? Would you be able to live surrendered to him if no one ever noticed? Can you trust that God is so very pleased with you, just as you are, and that his invitation is to a full life where the Spirit of God shapes you, more and more, in every little thing, to resemble our Savior, Jesus? Would you be convinced that the image of God in you, right where you are, is enough to make a difference for good and for God in the place God has you right now?

You don't need to move to another country. You don't need to speak in front of huge crowds. You don't need to stay where you are. You don't need to do it the way everyone else is doing it.

Can you find a way to release the hold you've got on your dreams and your plans for your life? Can you trust that God has got the best offer going, even if it looks like nothing more than shoveling mulch into a blue wheelbarrow and wheeling that mulch from the driveway behind your house to the flower bed in front of your house? Can you let that be holy work? Can it be sacred and offered up as worship to the one who takes great delight in you? Can you celebrate with God as the pile of mulch in your driveway grows smaller and smaller, and can you partner with God in the invitation to co-create with him by cultivating the small patch of earth beneath your feet?

But also . . .

Could you find a way, at a moment's notice, to release the accolades and the rave reviews and the bestseller lists on which your latest project now sits? Can you trust that the praise of people pales in comparison to the voice of God on that last day, whispered in your ear as he hugs you close, saying, "Well done." Can you stand in the middle of the spotlight's glow and remember that spotlight has an off switch and that switch is out of your control? Could you remember it's all about shining the spotlight on God?

Saying yes to God doesn't mean you'll suddenly be crystal clear about what to do next. It doesn't even mean you'll be able to tell the difference between God inviting you to try something and your own voice in your head. Saying yes doesn't mean that all of the things you attempt, all of the paths you take, all of the work to which you put your hand will be successful from the world's perspective. Sometimes the only way to see if something works is to give it a try. Sometimes you will have no doubts about the way God is leading you, or if he's leading you at all. Other times, you'll feel as if you're groping around in the dark, or you'll start to feel God may have misled you.

With each step, be mindful that what God is after is more of you. Nothing is lost in his economy. He turns logic and reason on its head, and just when it seems all is lost, he raises the dead and gives new life to everyone.

Don't be fooled. We are the lucky ones. Yes. Us. We, who are loved by God exactly the way we are. We are the lucky ones. The invitation couldn't be more clear. The voice of God breaks through the chaos, and the excellency of the power is of God and not of us, and it is so magnificent that it slips through

179

and into the very fiber of our beings so that we have to still our hearts and catch our breath and trust that light scatters the darkness every time. Then, when we find ourselves in the midst of deep silence, with our beaten and battered and everyday lives resting in the palm of his hand, we hear his whisper over us and in us and through us, and it is in this instant we find ourselves with our toes butted up against the threshold.

"Let there be . . . ," we hear him whisper over us.

We might choose not to step forward and accept God's invitation. We might not be convinced that one small step might make a difference, even if we don't see it. We might not move a single inch. But if we do . . .

Oh, if we do! If we can find it in ourselves to let go of ourselves and surrender ourselves; if we can become empty vessels before him—unwrapped and small—we invite him in and we give him permission (by the surrendering of our will to his, agreeing that he is God and we are not, and his plans for us are good, and he has already made it so) to lead us into the deep and glorious places right beneath our feet.

We will either step over the threshold or we won't. If we don't, God will love us, but we will still be holding on to what we've dreamed up on our own, and we will never know the power of God to work a miracle in our very own darkness and out of our very own nothing.

Ex nihilo.

God will save the day. God *has* saved the day. He can be trusted to pull the rip cord and also to keep you from drowning. He is love, and he can't help it. He's calling to you from just beyond the drop-off, and he is also standing right by your side. Exhale, and keep your chin up. He is your life, in every little thing.

Acknowledgments

It is impossible to write a book without a community of people cheering and praying and encouraging the author onward every single step of the way.

Thank you to Holley Gerth and Stephanie Bryant, who gave me my very first opportunity to write as part of an online community. Your belief in me was a complete surprise and an unexpected gift, one I will treasure forever.

Brad, Michelle, Noah, and Rowan, Nebraska would not be home without you. Thank you for being our family on the Great Plains. Thank you for meals around the table and for long conversations in the living room. Thank you for bike rides and James Taylor and for scones and calzones. Thank you for loving us well and for making us laugh loudly and with wild abandon. Thank you for walking beside us in the most difficult days and for celebrating the brightest milestones. It's no coincidence that our two families ended up together beneath that great expanse of sky. Welcome to the good life. Peace.

Jennifer, Scott, Anna, and Lydia, and also Phil and Mama D., you gave me a safe place to land at just the right moment. Thank you for opening your home to me. The time I spent there will always serve as a touchstone and a reminder not to throw in the towel, not to let discouragement win out, and not to give up on God's desire to tear down the walls we build up to keep each other at a distance.

Shelly Miller, your voice rings in my ears like the sweetest melody. You inspire hope, and you ground that hope in truth. Thank you for your generosity in sharing wisdom and for the way you refuse to tiptoe around the truth. Thank you for not giving pat answers. Thank you for drawing goodness out of a person. Out of me. You are a bright light in this world.

Ann Voskamp, thank you for leaning in, right from the start. I love you, girlfriend.

Lisa-Jo Baker, your wit and wisdom win the day. You lead well, and I am pleased to follow and learn from you.

Ann Kroeker, thank you for your insight, your wisdom, and your wit.

Carolyn McCready, Andrea Doering, and Laura Barker, you each saw something in me that I wasn't even looking for. Thank you for your steady encouragement, not just for me but also for all the authors whose messages you help send out to the world. You are stellar, each of you.

HC Prayer Warriors, not everyone gets to have a crew like you in her life. Who knew what would come of a weekend together by the Frio River? Thank you for being a rock in a weary land and a solid foundation for me.

Acknowledgments

Marcus Goodyear, Katie Cherniss, and the HC team, it's an honor to serve God with you. You make me a deeper thinker, a closer disciple of Jesus, a better writer, and a fine player of Two Truths and a Lie. Thank you for being such a strong team, committed to following God into your high calling.

To my (in)courage sisters: You are the most savvy, sweet, sassy, sophisticated, sincere, smart, silly, Spirit-led, and Spirit-filled group of women I have ever met. You make me believe deep and wonderful things about community and God and hope and grace, and about me.

To The Book Club. You know who you are, and I am better because of you. Thank you for pressing through.

FBCL, you are my people. Thank you for not giving up. Thank you for potlucks and praise teams and Spaghetti Thursdays. Thank you for sharing your stories and for believing in mine. Thank you for holding out to see what the end will be. We are in this together, and for the long haul.

Jen, Ruth, and Stacey, thank you for walking with me on this journey. Your friendship has been the perfect gift at just the right time.

The *Jumping Tandem* community, you carried me through. Way back in 2008, when I wrote my very first online piece, I had no idea where this would lead. And you have stuck with me, every step of the way. Thank you for showing up to read and comment. Thank you for sharing my words with your friends and among your communities. Thank you for retreating with me in Nebraska. You are the most generous, real, talented, and faithfully committed people I know. I'll see you in the comment box.

Bill Jensen, you are masterful and you serve well. Thank you for having my best interests at heart and for honoring my heart at the same time. You led well and didn't let me get lost in the process.

Rebekah Guzman, thank you for stewarding my words well. Thank you for helping me get to the heart of the matter and for hanging tough with me through the weeds. It is a blessing to have been partnered with you.

To the team at Baker, I'm so grateful for your belief in this project, your hard work in tending to the details, and your patience with me as I found my way.

To Congressman John Lewis, thank you for getting me through the very last phase of writing this book. Right when I thought all hope was lost, your words found their way to me. I will be forever indebted to you, not just for the impact you had on me in the last two weeks of putting the words on the page but for your lifetime of service, your gentle but strong leadership, your commitment to lifting up the very best in people, and your faithful example through every season of your life.

Mom and Dad, you're the best parents a girl could ever ask for. Thanks for music and stories and dinner together and ballet lessons and bike rides and road trips and grace. Thank you for taking me to church and praying for me and introducing me to Jesus. Thank you for love that is fierce and strong and sweet and soft. I'll love you forever.

Christopher, Karen, Donovan, and Kyla, I love you from the bottom of my heart, all the way from Nebraska to Virginia and back again. Hold your dreams loosely and know that God sees you. God is for you. And so am I.

Jordan and Alexandra, you are my favorites. Forever and always, amen. If I started writing just how much I love and appreciate you, I don't know if I'd ever be able to stop—or to express it the way I feel it. You are the very best thing I have ever done. That will always be the truth, no matter what. My love for you surprises me—it is so deep and strong and light and lovely. Through thick and thin, at our very best and when we don't see eye to eye, I will always and ever swoon at the thought of you. You make me glad to be alive, and I am so proud to watch you live into every little thing your life will bring. Live life with gusto and don't be afraid of the drop-off. God takes great delight in you, and I'm in line right behind him.

Harry, you are my favorite person of all time. I'll tell you the rest over dinner.

Notes

Chapter 1 When You Miss the Mark

1. Anne Lamott, *Traveling Mercies: Some Thoughts on Faith* (New York: Anchor Books, 2000), 143.

Chapter 5 Breathlessness

1. James W. Johnson, *The Book of American Negro Poetry* (Harcourt, Brace, 1922), 117–120.

2. Oswald Chambers, *My Utmost For His Highest*, online daily devotional, November 10, 2014, http://utmost.org/fellowship-in-the -gospel/. Accessed January 26, 2015.

Chapter 6 Pay Attention

1. "Statement by Attorney General Robert F. Kennedy on departure from Poland," July 1, 1964, text available from the United States Department of Justice, http://www.justice.gov/ag/speeches-25. Accessed March 28, 2015.

Chapter 8 Every Little Thing

1. Bill Peel and Walt Larimore, *Workplace Grace: Becoming a Spiritual Influence at Work*, R. G. LeTourneau 125th Birthday Edition, (Longview, TX: LeTourneau Press, 2014), 71–72.

2. S.v. "*'amats*," in *Gesenius' Hebrew and Chaldee Lexicon to the Old Testament Scriptures*, trans. Samuel Tregelles (London: Samuel Bagster, nd), available at http://www.blueletterbible.org/lang/Lexicon /Lexicon.cfm?Strongs=H553&t=KJV.

3. Used by permission of Sandra Shelton.

Deidra Riggs is a writer and speaker. As founder of *Jumping Tandem*, Deidra leads an online community offering inspiration, encouragement, and a safe place to practice grace. She serves as managing editor at TheHighCalling.org, and she is a regular contributor to the (in)courage online community and an advocate for Help One Now. She lives in Lincoln, Nebraska, with her husband, Harry, and their dog, Santana. Connect with Deidra at www.deidrariggs.com.